CRYSTALS AND STONES

A COMPLETE GUIDE
TO THEIR HEALING PROPERTIES

The Group of 5

Paume de Saint-Germain Publishing
Montreal, Quebec, Canada

North Atlantic Books
Berkeley, California

Published by
Paume de Saint-Germain Publishing
235 Rene Levesque Boulevard East, Suite 310
Montreal, Quebec, H2X 1N8

and
North Atlantic Books
P.O. Box 12327
Berkeley, California 94712

Photography by B. Simhananda, Gaétan A. Brouillard
Book design by Lucie Létourneau, Lucie Robitaille
Illustration by Joani Gagnon
Typesetting by Lucie Létourneau, Louise Roy
Translated from the original French version by Kristiane Roy
Cover design by Susan Quasha
Cover photo © Bromand <http://www.dreamstime.com/Bromand_info> |
    Dreamstime.com <http://www.dreamstime.com/
Printed in the United States of America

Crystals and Stones: A Complete Guide to their Healing Properties is sponsored by the Society for the Study of Native Arts and Sciences, a nonprofit educational corporation whose goals are to develop an educational and cross-cultural perspective linking various scientific, social, and artistic fields; to nurture a holistic view of arts, sciences, humanities, and healing; and to publish and distribute literature on the relationship of mind, body, and nature.

PLEASE NOTE: The creators and publishers of this book disclaim any liabilities for loss in connection with following any of the practices, exercises, and advice contained herein. To reduce the chance of injury or any other harm, the reader should consult a professional before undertaking this or any other martial arts, movement, meditative arts, health, or exercise program. The instructions and advice printed in this book are not in any way intended as a substitute for medical, mental, or emotional counseling with a licensed physician or healthcare provider.

North Atlantic Books' publications are available through most bookstores. For further information, visit our Web site at www.northatlanticbooks.com or call 800-733-3000.

Library of Congress Cataloging-in-Publication Data

Crystals and stones : a complete guide to their healing properties / The Group of 5.
    p. cm.
  Includes index.
  Summary: "New Age readers will love this definitive guide to more than 190 stones and crystals and their impact on the physical, emotional, mental, and spiritual well being of individuals"—Provided by publisher.
  ISBN 978-1-55643-918-6
1. Crystals—Therapeutic use. 2. Stone—Therapeutic use. I. 5, The Group of.
  RZ415.C79 2010
  615.8'56—dc22

                                                            2010004017

1 2 3 4 5 6 7 8 9 SHERIDAN 15 14 13 12 11 10

We dedicate this book to Dadi Darshan Dharma, our precious guide in this present incarnation. He has transmitted to us his love for the mysterious kingdom of stones and crystals, and has shown us how to work in their company with respect and authenticity.

We also thank all our friends and patients who have allowed us to deepen our knowledge of this wondrous mineral kingdom that contains vast mysteries, which we hope one day to reveal.

CONTENTS

STONES, CRYSTALS, AND THERAPEUTIC PROPERTIES 47

* Photos of the stones and crystals portrayed in this book that do not have an asterisk below them come from the Lux Æterna Collection, located at 235 Rene Levesque Blvd. East, Suite 310, Montreal, Quebec, H2X 1N8, Canada.

FOREWORD

We could not give life to these pages without including an invocation on stones. It was written by Dadi Darshan Dharma as a tribute to the mineral kingdom. We recite it regularly, since it invites us never to forget that stones and crystals are great work companions that sustain us daily in the duty we are accomplishing towards humanity. They reveal themselves as perfect servants, devoted and thoughtful, that give their energy and power so that people may better meet their challenges in the diverse domains of their existence.

This book has been written thanks to the collaboration of the therapists at the Medicine Buddha Mandala Institute of Applied Alternative Therapies, located in Montreal since 2003. The institute distinguishes itself by a therapeutic approach that is a tribute to humanity with the help of the mineral kingdom.

Associated with the Lux Æterna Collection, which is the largest crystal collection in North America, the institute dispenses treatments in harmony with the different energetic bodies of a person. Its therapists have a solid training that allows them to manipulate stones and crystals while always respecting the personality and the physical, psychological, and emotional health of each individual.

The use of stones and crystals is in harmony with a modern therapeutic generation that is beginning to unveil the possibilities in this newly inaugurated Age of Aquarius, which will be more complete and more respectful of Universal Laws. Do we as humans share a secret with the minerals that constitute us? Do we not maintain a privileged link with them? Is this shared energy a bearer of incontestable benefit? Our answer: yes. While the benefits of treatments with stones and crystals are remarkable, we wish to emphasize that they should in no way replace traditional medicine, which remains essential for the treatment of many medical cases. We work in conjunction with physicians and never underestimate the extraordinary work they accomplish. This book is a response to the demand from our clientele to learn more about the mineral kingdom. It is the first in a series of seven volumes that will be devoted to the different aspects of the fascinating world of stones and crystals.

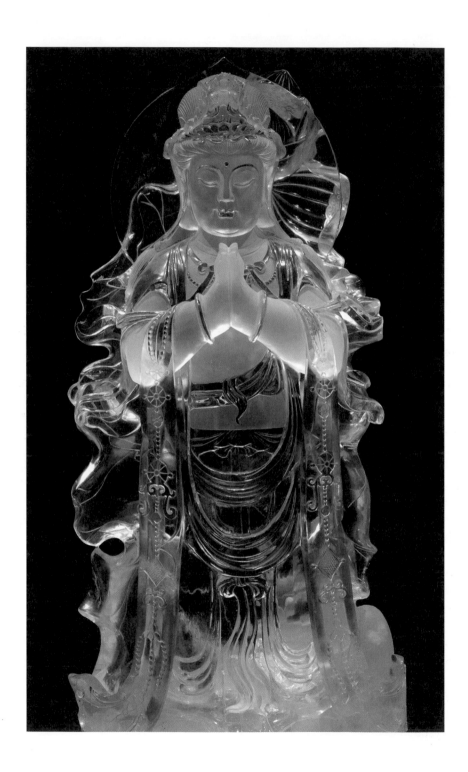

INVOCATION

I

Kinship of the Stone

IN THE BEGINNING two Sacred Loadstones from the Great Central Sun
Broke reverently into the Void of Cosmos, and coming irresistibly
together,

Brought to birth within its One Clap the sound of the Rainbow into Creation.

And it was upon the same Mythical Moment of mysterious Mystical Twine
That a lonely and lovely gemstone was instantly Agni-ized as planet Earth.

And chosen it was to be paramountly perched as a brilliant Blue Pearl
upon the deep indigo Necklace of Infinity.

And therewith began the Kinship of the Stone with the humming
Harmony of the Spheres.

Upon This Stone...

OF OLD, STONES WERE said to be the shattered bones of the gods.

He who won the Hermetic Stone epitomized Divine Power and Perfect Love.

He who accessed the Philosopher's Stone possessed the Truth and banished all Ignorance.

It was upon tablets of stone that were writ in flame the Ten Commandments by the finger of the Nameless One.

And there was placed beside each commandment a glowing gem, each being dropped selectively into the deep sapphire sea of a man's Being.

And there issued forth in the Medieval era the Wondrous Work of the Alchemical Stone; and there was the Singing Stone of the Wise Man; and there was the Knight Templar of the Golden Stone, riding his steed of righteousness into the "terra incognito" of the Masonic Square.

And there was the quintessential quest for the gem-studded, oracular chalice of the Holy Grail, enfolding the living waters and loving attar of life eternal.

And there was, and is, the Kaaba Monolith of mystical and traditional Islam, once blissfully white, and now blackened over eons by the bittersweet tears of long-suffering pilgrims and the salacious stain of sin.

And lead, to the Egyptians, led unerringly to the skeleton of Saturn; and iron was about the muscled marrow of Mars, and silver gave shine to the Moon, and antimony bravely braced up the Earth.

And of shining stone and jubilant gem was the glow and the glory of the once Great Pyramid.

And each planet of the Zodiac is gem potentized, and each constellation is gem consecrated, and each of the Seven Solar Men stands gem-authorized before the Diamond Throne of the Lord of Shamballa.

And that mythical stone, the "Heliogabalus," also black, was said to be especially sacred to the Sun.

Conjecture claims, (perhaps), that it was teleported down Jacob's Ladder, and became the infamous Black Rock pillow, upon which this extraordinary Servant of God laid his head in rest every eve.

And which now, in occult and humble fashion, adorns the seat of the eminent coronation chair in the Abbey of Westminster.

And finally it was once said (not so long ago) that: "Upon this stone, I shall build my Church...," and thus again was reaffirmed the sacred kinship of stone and Spirit.

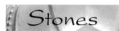

Stones

STONES BREATHE DEEPLY in patient beauty and grow in studied symmetry.

Slowly, they exhale their light in perfect and unreserved service to all, whether the all be that of the universe, or a planet, or simply the kingdom of mineral, plant, animal, or man.

Stones are spiritual carriers of the principle of growth, of elevation, of evolution.

They arouse the winds of change to cast their vibratile incorporiality upon the samsaric consciousness.

Slowly, slowly, stones correct all wrong thinking and do their best to amplify the philosophic perspective.

And empower do they, the imprisoned small-self, to have Divine concourse with the bright awesomeness of the Soul.

IV

Gemstones

A GEMSTONE'S HEART beats slowly, pulses highly, and never forgets the lowly.

A gemstone's roots are elemental but devic in essence, and earthly bent in daily task.

A gemstone comes from the light, is made of light, and is a bearer of light to World upon worlds of shadow and distress, doubt and despair, woe and wrong.

A gemstone is the eye of the sky casting a pure look through the dust of conflict and pain.

A gemstone is the distillation of heaven's Love aesthetically cast in crystalline concentration upon all human cry and call.

To pick up and pocket a gemstone is to self-create a covenant for conversion, commutation, and change.

To pick up and pocket a gemstone is to decide to truncate and temper all struggle and strife.

To pick up and pocket a gemstone is to beckon a holy helper to come renew our resolve and restore our strength.

To pick up and pocket a gemstone is to honor the hand of the mineral kingdom and to dine with the Divine in variegated hues of adamantine Light.

V

Blessed Be the Stone

BLESSED BE THE STONE... for in it is to be found the Gem of God.

BLESSED BE THE STONE... for in it is grounded the Brilliance of God.

BLESSED BE THE STONE... for in it is built the Beauty of God.

BLESSED BE THE STONE... for in it is shaped the Geometry of God.

BLESSED BE THE STONE... for in it is organized the Chemistry of God.

BLESSED BE THE STONE... for in it is set the Adamantine Word of God.

BLESSED BE THE STONE... for in it is held the Wisdom of God.

BLESSED BE THE STONE... for in it is housed the Harmony of God.

BLESSED BE THE STONE... for in it is honored the Healing Angel of God.

BLESSED BE THE STONE... for in it is affixed the Mercy of God.

BLESSED BE THE STONE... for in it is crouched the Grace of God.

BLESSED BE THE STONE... for in it is fructified the Benevolence of God.

BLESSED BE THE STONE... for in it is inspirited the Intelligence of God.

BLESSED BE THE STONE... for in it is forged the Power of God.

BLESSED BE THE STONE... for in it is matrixed the Love of God.

BLESSED BE THE STONE... for in it is substantiated the Science of God.

BLESSED BE THE STONE... for in it is conjured the Magnificent Magus of God.

BLESSED BE THE STONE... for in it is "humanized" the Light of God.

BLESSED BE THE STONE... for in it is dreamt the Dream of God.

BLESSED BE THE STONE... for in it is inscribed the Plan of God.

BLESSED BE THE STONE... for in it is encoded the Purpose of God.

BLESSED BE THE STONE... for in it is envisioned Man's Service to God.

BLESSED BE THE STONE... for in it is salaamed Man's Devotion to HIM.

Dadi Darshan Dharma
October 20–21, 2004

INTRODUCTION

Stones and crystals have been fascinating humanity for thousands of years. They have been tools of work and transformation for humanity ever since we discovered their existence and realized their potential.

Whether you are wandering around Paris, London, Kathmandu, or Beijing, you cannot escape their influence. Stones and crystals are everywhere, and their uses are multiple. The Tibetan master D. K. mentions that in terms of their appearance, crystals represent the divine plan that is hidden in their perfect geometry and that the radiant beauty of God is condensed in the radiant color of precious stones.

If we could follow the step-by-step transformation of coal into diamond, we would discover what enabled prince Siddhartha to "awaken" and become the Being of Light known to this day as the Buddha. The kingdom of stones and crystals evolves in parallel to our own, giving life, in each era, to new species that have the mission to sustain humanity in its transformation. Thus, we can now find quartz strewn with Tibetan stupas, "ocelot" quartz, "ajoite" quartz, and many other types of quartz that permit a person who sincerely desires it to evolve further and more rapidly towards his or her destiny.

Ajoite

Ocelot

It is important to choose these companions well, as they sustain us in what we have to accomplish. Some will be very effective in maintaining our physical health, while others will adjust our emotional body so that it remains solid while facing life's hazards.

HOW STONES WORK

The way energy exchange is produced between stones and human beings remains a profound mystery that many have tried to elucidate. One scientific theory explains that while the patient is undergoing treatment, an interaction is produced at the level of the cutaneous tissues, when the dermal enzymes in contact with the stone carry out a chemical exchange that is then transferred into the blood stream. Thus, thanks to this exchange, the minerals in the stone travel in the blood and nourish the organs in need, promptly giving them the nutritious elements they lack. This theory would explain the important health improvement in the individual being treated in lithotherapy.

However, how can we explain the effect generated upon the emotional body of a person, since a remarkable improvement is also often noted at this level? Of course, certain minerals help preserve emotional equilibrium, which partly answers our question. But how can a stone ease the suffering of a broken heart or of an individual in mourning so rapidly? Furthermore, how can we explain how a stone diminishes the electromagnetic effects produced upon the physical body when the body is placed near a computer?

Certain research points to the fact that stones emit energy that affects the physical body of human beings by means of resonance. Placed upon an acupuncture point, the stone "resonates" a vibratory note, thus stimulating this precise point which, by intermediary of the meridian to which it is affiliated, permits the organ to restore itself.

How, then, does the stone's color play an equally important role in this process? For example, blue stones will be beneficial to the throat region, while pink stones will be beneficial to the heart region. We believe it is possible that stones possess an "auric" field, just like human beings, and that these fields communicate with the help of nadis. Defined as energetic channels, of which the meridians are part, nadis transmit their energy to the chakras, which then affect the glands and organs to which they are affiliated. Those who have the capacity to see these energetic fields note that the union between these two fields increases the auric quality of the individual, raising the possibility of a transfer from the stone's "aura" to that of the treated person. This communion permits the stone to give of itself in order to create balance and harmony where there is distress.

This symbiosis could explain the degradation of certain stones that "work" and "give" of themselves without reserve. While some maintain that stones are inert, without life, how is it that they have the possibility to grow or to deteriorate? How can a crack or a marked discoloration following a therapy session be interpreted? No one can really answer this question. We can only assert that we have witnessed "little inexplicable miracles" in operation and that this magic never ceases to amaze us.

HARDNESS OF STONES AND CRYSTALS

We have noticed that stone hardness plays an important role in their energetic work. Stones that have a superior hardness value "transfer and emit" while stones that are qualified as softer "absorb and purify." Stones with a hardness level above four will have a tendency to emit energy, while stones with an equal or lesser hardness value will have a tendency to absorb.

For example, when dealing with a wound, the therapist will work with a malachite, a very absorbent stone, that will soak up the "inflammation."

It is important to mention that "absorbent" stones are more fragile and must rest on a human body for only a short time. Ten minutes will be sufficient; the therapist will then be able to replace it with a stone that will emit beneficial energy, such as an emerald, to promote cellular regeneration.

CHOOSING STONES AND CRYSTALS

There are many levels at which stones and crystals have an influence. A stone or crystal can treat physical pain, reduce an existential uneasiness, or guide on a spiritual path. The choice of a stone or crystal therefore takes on a significant importance, since the conveyed energy will have repercussions on many aspects of an individual's life. Beauty must not be the only criterion, since beauty is not necessarily synonymous with effectiveness.

It is said that it is often the stone that chooses us, and not the other way around. We can confirm that this is true in a majority of cases. When a stone or crystal attracts and fascinates us, there is a strong possibility that we have found the companion we were looking for. A mutual resonance is installed, creating a beneficial energetic bond. Our intuition remains our best ally, for neither cost nor beauty should be an obstacle to its acquisition.

FACTORS INFLUENCING STONE AND CRYSTAL PRICES

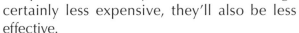

Many factors influence the price of a stone or crystal. First, the authenticity of the piece will play an important role in the utilization we'll make of it. An artificial turquoise, created in a laboratory, will not be as efficient as a real turquoise. So be wary of imitations: although certainly less expensive, they'll also be less effective.

Dow crystal

The purity of the piece is an equally important factor to consider when purchasing a stone or crystal. The more crystalline it is, the greater its capacity to convey light. It will transmit its therapeutic particularities in less time and will increase our chances of success.

The rarity of a stone or crystal directly influences its worth, hence its price. So, crystal from Tibet will be more expensive than crystal from Arkansas. The originality of a piece and the extent of its beauty are often considered criteria of rarity, which increase the value of a stone or crystal.

DIMENSIONS OF A STONE OR CRYSTAL

The choice of the dimensions of a stone or crystal depends on the use we wish to make of it. In therapy, we tend to choose smaller pieces that will be comfortable for the body. In daily life, certain pieces are ideally worn as jewelry. The dimensions and location (on the neck, finger, directly on the skin, or in the pocket) have a direct impact on the desired effect at the place where we wish it to be produced. As a decorative piece, or to harmonize and

increase the energy and light of a given area, it is advisable to favor more-imposing pieces like geodes or quartz clusters, which can be placed in a room, such as an office, or any other location.

CARE OF STONES AND CRYSTALS

Stones and crystals are precious friends; owing to their high sensitivity, proper care requires a particular vigilance that necessitates specific treatments. Ignoring this rule can lead to the destruction of these companions. When in doubt, it is better to refrain and wait to be certain as to the approach to be used. However, we have found two methods that are efficient and without danger: incense and an amethyst or quartz cluster.

Regarding incense, just pass it over the stone or crystal for a few minutes. Reciting a mantra may increase the purifying effects. The choice of a mantra is a personal one, but "OM" has proven to be as potent as a more elaborate mantra.

The use of a quartz or amethyst cluster is easy: it is simply a matter of letting the piece rest on the cluster for a few hours. The quartz or amethyst cluster will clean and charge the piece by injecting it with a supplementary energy dose that will render it more effective.

Several other cleaning methods are also available. However, we wish to reiterate that vigilance is important, since a bad choice can be fatal to your companion. Do not hesitate to consult books or to contact a specialist for advice on the best method to use for the stone or crystal you wish to clean.

BEST-KNOWN CLEANING METHODS

- sunlight, ideal for all quartz
- moonlight, preferred by kyanite
- fresh, cold water, adored by the majority of stones and crystals
- salt, to be used with caution
- earth, in certain cases, particularly if a crystal is very damaged
- snow, as a replacement for cold water

BEST-KNOWN RECHARGING METHODS

- quartz cluster
- sunlight
- moonlight
- cold water
- incense
- mantras

USING STONES AND CRYSTALS IN PERSONAL THERAPY

We can wear a stone or crystal as jewelry or directly on the body. Ideally, precious and semiprecious stones must touch the skin, but not all quartz families, among them crystals such as amethyst, citrine and others, require contact with the skin. These crystals and stones can be worn on our person, in cotton or linen pouches, or simply slipped in our pockets. For maximum efficiency, the piece must be located as close as possible to the area we wish to treat. It is better to wear one stone or crystal at a time; however, in certain cases, wearing a few pieces simultaneously can also be beneficial.

The length of time a stone or crystal should be worn differs depending upon the purpose and result desired; it can vary from a few minutes to a few hours. Generally, when worn as jewelry, we should let the stone or crystal rest for the night after we remove it. If we wear a crystal such as a citrine on our skin for a specific benefit (for example, to facilitate digestion) in general, the crystal should not be worn for more than a few hours. It is our duty to be attentive to our body and its reactions.

THERAPEUTIC METHODS USING STONES AND CRYSTALS

Here is a brief explanation of an easy and reliable method of using stones and crystals for short therapeutic sessions at home:

1. Choose stones or crystals with which you wish to work.

2. Retreat to a quiet place where you can lie down.

3. Place the stones and crystals near you.

4. Lie down on your back.

5. Place the stones or crystals on your body, starting with the root chakra, working your way up until you reach the crown chakra.

6. Rest for about twenty minutes, with or without music.

7 When the time has elapsed, remove the stones or crystals one at a time, starting with the piece located at the crown chakra.

8. Stay calm and still for about five to ten minutes before getting up.

9. Clean the stones or crystals using the appropriate method.

DISPOSITION OF STONES AND CRYSTALS ON THE BODY

The choice of where to place stones and crystals on the body is related to the pain or discomfort to be treated. The stone can be placed directly on the skin, on or near the affected organ or area in pain. In such a case, it is advised not to leave the stone or crystal at this location for more than twenty minutes at a time.

In order to maximize the effect of stones and crystals, it is beneficial to know their appropriate placement. Here is a general idea of the relationship between chakras, stones, and crystals. The recognition and application of this relationship can help to ease the discomforts associated with certain parts of the body more efficiently.

Root chakra (1st chakra)

Color of chakra: red

Color of stones: red, black, grey

Locations: base of the spinal column or the soles of the feet

Physical body: teeth, renal glands, legs, small and large intestines, feet, kidneys, skeleton, lymphatic system, bladder

Emotional body: relating to material comfort, grounding, will to live, nervous system

Indications: anemia, apathy, no sense of responsibility, constipation, difficulty relaxing, pain within the body, irritable bowels, irritability, lack of concentration, loss of energy, irrational fears, rage and anger, nervous disorders

Corresponding stones: red agate, red aventurine, garnet, hematite, red jasper, red tiger eye, fire opal, bloodstone, ruby, black tourmaline, zoisite

Hara chakra (2nd chakra)

Color of chakra: orange

Color of stones: orange, brown, beige, yellow, peach, gold

Location: lower abdomen, two fingers below navel

Physical body: gonads, sciatic nerve, lymphatic system, genito-urinary system

Emotional body: relating to the center of will and self-affirmation, creativity, sensuality

Indications: relationship difficulties, mood swings, frigidity and impotence, menopause, painful menstruation, fear of the sexual act, problems related to dependency on alcohol and tobacco, water retention, shyness

Corresponding stones: amber, orange calcite, citrine, coral, carnelian, copper, yellow sapphire, topaz

Solar plexus chakra (3rd chakra)

Color of chakra: yellow

Color of stones: yellow, green

Locations: sternum

Physical body: colon, stomach, liver, oesophagus, pancreas, small intestine, spleen, gallbladder, eyes

Emotional body: relating to anxiety, authoritarian attitude, need to always be right, depression, lack of combativeness, lack of courage and self-esteem, nervousness

Indications: inflexible attitude, depression, general fatigue, hyperactivity, food intolerance, lack of self-esteem, digestion problems, blood pressure imbalances, low immunity, sadness

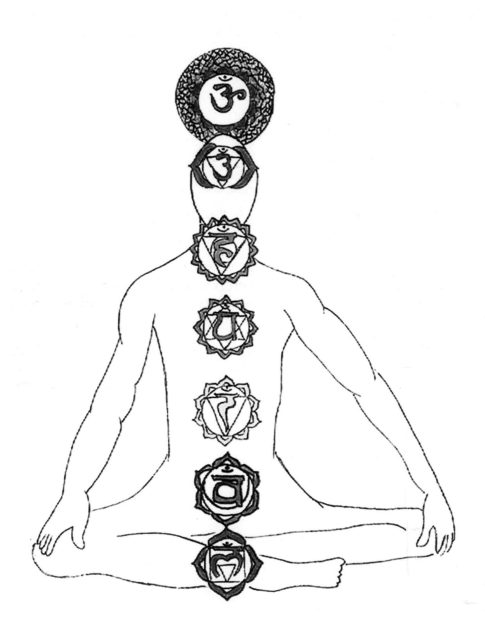

Corresponding stones: amber, ametrine, yellow calcite, green calcite, green fluorite, jade, malachite, tiger eye, sunstone, epidote quartz, smoky quartz, rutilated quartz, yellow sapphire, yellow topaz, yellow tourmaline

Heart chakra (4th chakra)

Color of chakra: green

Color of stones: green, pink

Location: chest center, between the breasts

Physical body: arms, heart, chest, lungs, thymus

Emotional body: relating to love and compassion

Indications: difficulty in expressing emotions; frequent relationship failures; emotional fragility; indifference to others; cardiac, cutaneous, immune- and blood-related illnesses; fear of loving; tendency to be abused; tendency to feel superior to others

Corresponding stones: moss agate, amazonite, aventurine, green calcite, chrysoprase, pink danburite, pink fluorite, green garnet (tsavorite, uvarovite), jade, green jasper, kunzite, malachite, moldavite, rose quartz, rhodochrosite, rhodonite

Throat chakra (5th chakra)

Color of chakra: blue

Color of stones: blue, green

Location: lower region of the throat

Physical body: mouth, bronchus, vocal cords, shoulders, thyroid gland, throat, tongue, nape, esophagus, ears

Emotional body: relating to communication, creative power

Indications: stammering; thyroid malfunction;, difficulty in expressing oneself; incoherent speech; discomfort related to ears, upper respiratory system, and larynx; awkward physical coordination; nervousness; tendency to dramatize facts

Corresponding stones: blue lace agate, aquamarine, azurite, chrysocolla, blue fluorite, kyanite, lapis lazuli, larimar, aqua aura quartz, sapphire, tanzanite, turquoise, blue topaz, amazonite

Third eye chakra (6th chakra)

Color of chakra: violet

Color of stones: violet, purple, mauve, indigo, blue

Location: between eyebrows

Physical body: pituitary gland (hypophysis), also affecting memory and intelligence, both brain hemispheres, ears, sinus, eyes

Emotional body: relating to the capacity to analyze, self-esteem, intuition

Indications: nightmares, difficulty facing the truth, self-centeredness, insomnia, headaches, lack of subtlety, neuralgia, fear of communicating, rejection of daily tasks, sinusitis, withdrawn personality, imbalances in endocrine system, metabolism troubles

Corresponding stones: amethyst, azurite, charoite, purple fluorite, iolite, lepidolite, sugulite, tanzanite, kyanite

Crown chakra (7th chakra)

Color of chakra: clear, white

Color of stones: clear, white, violet, gold

Locations: summit of cranium

Physical body: brain, pineal gland (epiphysis)

Emotional body: relating to the connection to the higher self

Indications: headaches, immune system deficiency, psychomotor problems, dogmatism, fanaticism, exaggerated mysticism, mental rigidity

Corresponding stones: ametrine, danburite, diamond, clear fluorite, herkimer, pearl, clear quartz, white sapphire, selenite, white topaz

THE CRYSTAL

A crystal's life cycle is, in itself, a powerful representation of human evolution; from a state of passive original carbon, it undergoes multiple transmutations and evolves into a radioactive product: a living incandescence in earth's igneous womb. The final result is often extraordinary due to its inherent beauty. The bursting clarity of a crystal seems to instantaneously silence the rational mind full of judgments and fears, forcing the individual to reside in the simplicity of the present moment.

In his thought-provoking book *The Smiling Forehead: Paradoxes from Dadi to Daughter*, Dadi Darshan Dharma speaks these words of wisdom: "Do not speak of radiant beauty without Divine Presence."[1] Those who have been deeply touched, even once, by the beauty of crystals know that the Divine truly resides on earth.

Crystals are lighthouses of high-frequency energy. They intervene energetically by injecting white light to dissolve etheric blockages. They work on the subtle bodies, which reflect themselves in the aura field. They can literally "de-crystallize" rigid blockages, gradually releasing stagnant energies with the potential to liberate ancient patterns that perpetuate suffering and ignorance. A conscious working relationship with the right crystal can increase our inner light, thereby awakening a clearer vision and a greater balance, with the potential for an expansion of consciousness.

---

1. Dadi Darshan Dharma, *The Smiling Forehead: Paradoxes from Dadi to Daughter*, Montreal: Orange Palm and Magnificent Magus Publications, 2007, 193.

A crystal whose essence is awakened becomes a powerful companion on the spiritual path. Choosing to merge and interact with a crystal's inhabiting energy with awareness and respect can awaken the intuition, deepen one's meditation, and facilitate recovery and self-purification.

CHANNELER

The Channeler exhibits a seven-sided main face and a back face in the form of a triangle.

The Channeler favors the descent of energies of higher vibratory frequencies into the physical. As its name suggests, this crystal teaches us how to become "channelers" of divine energy. It helps to establish contact with the source of divine knowledge, with the masters or guides, in order to discover and understand the way or the path to life. This crystal represents the spiritual student or the seeker on the path.

It is important to be adequately prepared and well-centered before using such a crystal. It is recommended to inwardly ask for protection so as to invite only higher energies that will prove beneficial for ourselves as well as for humanity.

TRANSMITTER

A Transmitter crystal can be identified as having two seven-sided faces at the terminal end of the crystal, separated by a triangle. It symbolizes the quality of expression untainted by the desires of the lower self.

In numerology, the "seven" symbolizes introspection, spiritual awareness, and higher knowledge. It represents a profound knowing and exploring of oneself and the universe. It allows us to apply a mental analysis to higher truths, grounding spirit into matter.

The three-sided triangle allows for verbalization of these higher truths. It represents creative expression of inner thoughts and feelings. It urges us to express the joy of living in the present moment regardless of how that moment is qualified. The 7:3:7 ratio allows us to communicate wisdom and higher truths to the material world.

We are presently merging into the Aquarian age, welcoming the advent of the Ray 7 energy, whose ultimate destiny is the manifestation of spirit into matter. Humanity is therefore called to be consistently tuned into the inner while consciously working in the outer world. The time for private spiritual retreats and isolation from others is over, and the age of group sharing, teaching, and evolution is taking precedence.

The Transmitter crystal can help us build the bridge from the inner to the outer, while still remaining centered and grounded. Before meditating with this crystal, it is important to ask for protection and guidance. Surround yourself with white light and ask that only the highest good comes from whatever connection may be made from the session. You may hold the crystal in your receiving hand (left if right-handed and vice versa), and then place the seven-sided face at your third-eye or heart chakra. You may also visualize blue light at your throat chakra and violet light at your third eye while staying calm and receptive.[2] Clarity, balance and positive intentions are a must, and with persistent practice, the Transmitter crystal can become an invaluable companion.

DOW OR TRANS-CHANNELING CRYSTAL

The formation of the Dow crystal can be summarized as "7-3-7-3-7-3" due to its three faces with seven sides and its three triangular faces that separate each of the seven-sided faces. The Dow is known to be geometrically perfect, as it combines the properties of both the Channeler and the Transmitter crystals. This particular geometric configuration emits the highest and most powerful vibration of the mineral kingdom. It is said that the Dow is the crystal that has attained the highest degree of evolution. It conveys the reality of spiritual perfection into the world of matter and can serve as a guide throughout the process of inner growth.

The Dow is also a crystal of creativity. It facilitates the connection between the heart and mind, since it is through the union of divine compassion and spiritual knowledge that illumination and conscious action can be manifested for the well-being of the planet and its inhabitants.

The Dow has the power to activate the heart chakra, hence guiding the individual toward an expression of authentic love and compassion. Its powerful therapeutic action allows one to feel in intimate resonance with the energy of divine love.

---

[2] RAPHAELL, *Crystal Healing.*

ENGRAVED CRYSTAL

The Engraved crystal is quite rare. Hieroglyphs or engraved writings, which come from the past, from the future, or from parallel worlds, can be found inside the crystal or on its surface. The information contained within the crystal allows its user to contact these other worlds or dimensions and connect with a certain wisdom or knowledge that has disappeared or become inaccessible.

The Engraved crystal is different from its cousins, the Time Link and the Record Keeper, due to its content, which is more specific in the type of information revealed. These writings can be compared to sacred mantras, carriers of energy of transformation.

The Engraved crystal is a powerful tool that must be solely utilized for humanitarian, and therefore nonpersonal, goals. It is recommended that the user be the only one to work with the crystal, for the energy contained in it could be destroyed or rendered inaccessible were it to be used by a misinformed user.

Because it has the power to heal, the Engraved crystal should be used with discernment so as not to impede the personal or collective karma of those who need its help.

ISIS

The name "Isis" has been assigned to a particular type of crystal in honor of the Egyptian goddess of the same name. Isis has been revered in Egypt as an icon of true feminine power, yet many cultures and religions have venerated female deities who embody the same principles of the "divine feminine"; whether it be Tara from Tibetan Buddhism, Quan Yin from China, Mary from the Christian faith or Mahalakshmi from the Hindu religion. She may have many faces, yet she embodies the same principles of love, surrender, creation, and profound healing.

The "Isis" symbol on a crystal can be identified as having five sides forming one of the faces. The number five in numerology is the number of the "human soul," having incarnated on the physical plane in order to experience the world of duality, with all of its intense pains and pleasures, through the limitations of the five senses. The "five" encourages one eventually to resolve the opposing forces, to come to a deeper understanding and a just vision of the events in life that are the cause of such pleasure and of so much suffering. It offers the opportunity to embrace life in its wholeness, the good and the bad, rather than limiting our perception and understanding to the five senses.

The Isis symbol is a key to integrating and transcending personal pain and suffering; it represents freedom through change and transformation. This change can be brought about through making a conscious decision to alter the way we see and live life, to transform the way we have narrowly perceived our trials and tribulations throughout our earthly existence.

The energy of the earth or matter itself is known to be feminine in its polarity, while the sky or "spirit" masculine. Movement must eventually be made to unify spirit and matter, to embody and live according to the universal spiritual laws while living the full gamut of earthly experience. This will eventually lead to an inner unity while living in a world of duality. In other words, the reality of our "divine soul" will manifest amongst the density of the physical plane. We thereby live consciously; we become fluid, malleable, and receptive channels of light and love. We become the compassionate beings that we see reflected in the icons that we revere.

The following story shows us that it is possible to heal ourselves as we surrender to the love force that flows through all of Creation. It tells of freedom through change and transformation.

THE LEGEND OF ISIS

Isis loved and married her brother Osiris, who was good and just, and together they ruled Egypt. Their brother Seth was jealous and cruel, and he secretly plotted against Osiris, seeking to usurp his leadership.

While Isis was away, Osiris invited many guests, including Seth, to a banquet held at his residence. Seth built a coffin that fit Osiris', proportions precisely and brought it to the banquet. Seth pretended it was a gift for someone else, and created a game, daring the guests to climb inside and see if they could fit. Of course, noone could, and Osiris good-humoredly took his turn. As expected, he fit perfectly, at which point Seth slammed the lid shut and poured molten lead over the coffin, suffocating Osiris to death. The coffin was thrown into the ocean and Seth took over the kingdom.

When Isis returned and learned what had happened, she went half mad with grief and fell into emotional despair. She retreated to the island of Algika, where she went into a deep depression. One day, Hathor, the goddess of love, appeared by her side, and Isis laid her head on her bosom, receiving much love and nurturing. She drew great strength from Hathor and eventually regained her personal power. Following many struggles, she finally bore a son, Horus, who eventually took down Seth and restored justice to the land. Had Isis closed herself off from Hathor's energy, she never would have found her true power, she never would have "created" Horus, who eventually conquered the evil forces ruling the land.

The ideals of the divine feminine are quickly re-emerging into the collective consciousness of humanity, bringing with them balance and wholeness. Isis is a powerful catalyst for integration and change, for both men and women alike.

RECORD KEEPER

The Record Keeper can be recognized as one or more raised triangles on the face of a crystal. These triangles are like data banks that have stored incredible amounts of information, programmed by ancient beings of various civilizations throughout the earth's history.

These crystals have been consciously programmed with advanced healing techniques and higher knowledge to aid in the expansion of consciousness and the evolution of humankind. It is said that only the pure of heart and mind can have access to these data banks, yet these crystals will often commence a purification process in those who have attracted this kind of quartz, preparing them for the possibility of consciously attuning to the inner energies of the records.

The triangular shapes are like doors that lead to the "records" contained in the crystal. One can place them at the third eye while remaining receptive. They can also be rubbed with the thumb of the receptive hand (left for right-handed and vice versa) from top to bottom to access these "files," and then from bottom to top to close them.[3] One may receive intuitive images, symbols, innovative ideas, or energy frequencies that

[3]RAPHAELL, *Crystal Healing.*

may alter or propel ones growth. Knowledge may come in dreams, in meditation, or in more occulted forms, depending on the readiness, intentions, and openness of its user.

TIME LINK

The Time Link crystal exhibits a facet in the shape of a parallelogram that connects two of its other faces. Facing the crystal, if the parallelogram is situated at the left of a face, it acts as a link with past lives, whereas when it is situated at the right of a face, it becomes a link with future lives.

The Time Link acts as a bridge between who we once were and who we are called to become. Its principal goal is to help us evaluate our past and present, as well as our future potential, with a broader perspective, allowing us to resolve certain conflicts and heal undeniable wounds. Gradually, healing, forgiveness, and a sense of letting go will become possible, therefore allowing for better self-understanding and a unity of being.

The characteristics of both the Time Link and the Isis are sometimes found in the same crystal. This happy meeting confers to the crystal an even greater power for the process of healing.

WINDOW

The Window is actually a diamond shape connecting the face and the body of a crystal. The "window" does everything in its power to break down ego defenses, revealing its games and patterns, in order to dissipate delusions and pierce illusions.

It symbolizes the raw truth and is therefore very powerful as it purges and purifies the darkest aspects of our being. The "Window" acts as a mirror, revealing all the impurities reflected in our auras, which veil our true nature. We must therefore be prepared psychologically to face our shadow side, otherwise the ego can experience more than it can handle, and the process can be quite traumatic. While meditating, we can gaze into the diamond form, where it may project images of what may be impeding our growth. Once a purification of all that impedes clear vision is complete, the Window can guide us on an inner journey where our true Self resides. The lozenge will actually act as a screen where we may be able to see ourselves in action. It is often quite easy to judge others but very difficult to be honest with ourselves; the Window helps us with that process.

The symbolism of the number four represents learning to live with limitations, demands, and responsibilities of the physical plane. It teaches us not to fight against the flow and not to escape what life would like us to see and learn, but to accept what is there and to make a meaningful existence with it; it teaches us to be real and present. The "four" is also considered a sacred number by pythagoreans, since it represents stability, solidity, equilibrium, and achievement.

The Window is a potent catalyst for real growth and change. The question is: Are you ready to see the truth?

VARIETIES OF QUARTZ

CATHEDRAL LIGHTBRAIRIES

A cathedral is a place where God is acknowledged, and a library is a site of learning. Together, it is a place where one can gain spiritual knowledge. Cathedral Lightbrairies are made of a main crystal surrounded by one or many smaller crystals or "chambers." During the growth period, a "twinning" takes place, which is a kind of double rotation inside that produces steps, or "offshoots." Cathedrals are here to establish a higher frequency of energy on the physical plane. They seem to have a direct link to universal knowledge and even the akashic records. This is a crystal for group meditation exercises; it will attract like-minded individuals who ardently wish to aid humankind in an expansion of consciousness. Cathedral quartz is like an illumined instructor from which students may acquire priceless information and receive transmissions of high-frequency energies. They present an opportunity for pragmatic, creative, and cooperative group work, answering to a collective appeal for real change.

Chlorite is a green mineral resembling green clay that can be found on the surface of, or inside, a quartz crystal. It may be in the form of a cloud, a nebula, or a phantom. A fortunate collector may even find chlorite inclusions in stones such as, topaz, calcite, or danburite. Green has always been associated with greater health and well-being. It helps the organism vibrate at a higher level than disease, encouraging balance and homeostasis. Hospitals with a lot of green in the environment have been known to have fewer infections. Chlorite is known for its purifying agents and has a tendency to eliminate toxins and act as an analgesic that attacks infections and bacteria. It also helps to purify at the cellular level and is a good protective agent against environmental and chemical pollutants. It has also been known to help with tumors and growths.

The heart chakra, when viewed on the etheric body, is also green; it is situated between the shoulder blades and also vibrates at the center of the chest. Named "Quartz of Compassion" by Dadi Darshan Dharma, chlorite quartz stimulates the heart center and can open us up to the energy of compassion for ourselves as well as for others. It can help us to heal old wounds, to forgive, and to let go of the past, encouraging greater communion with our soul, which is collective in its consciousness and all love in its expression.

ELESTIAL QUARTZ

Elestial Quartz is commonly called "skeletal." It is also known as "alligator" and "*jacare.*" These names are a reference to the similarities between the geometry on the surface of the crystal and the skin of a reptile. Elestial Quartz was brought to earth to guide humanity through a process of purification and healing, thereby awakening its potential to contact its inherent divinity. This crystal expresses the substance of the physical level of being and is aligned with angelic vibrations. The exact meaning of the word "elestial" is "angel crystal." Elestial Quartz contains the knowledge of the pre-physical state and the comprehension of reincarnation. It offers great comfort in times of transition between life and death, helping one to let go of the fear of abandoning the physical body and giving access to the power to merge with the immortality of soul.

Resembling a human brain, this quartz will balance the frequency waves of the brain and neutralize thought forms that are inaccurate or confused. It activates the pineal gland, associated with the crown chakra, and creates the potential for expansion of consciousness. The nature of the Elestial connects one to the higher Self, to Truth, the Source, and the roots of existence. During the purification process, many obsolete identifications will need to be released in order to eventually lead to inner peace. The Elestial Quartz brings us to the heart of things, to the inner truth and the center of our being. It purifies any element that would prevent the expression of the true Self.

Elestials are potent catalysts for the purification of the darker aspects of our lower self, and it is therefore recommended to work wisely with these quartz. Choose the dimensions, size, and intensity carefully, and tune into the dosage and frequency that is right for you. It is also suggested to work with healing and balancing stones that can help integrate what the Elestial will impose. The Elestial Quartz is magical, particular, and quite rare. It calls a person once he or she is ready for an authentic confrontation with the naked truth.

FADEN QUARTZ

Faden Quartz is usually tabular-shaped or flat and elongated. A white line, or filament, runs through the middle of the quartz. This line is parallel with the direction of the tabular; it is usually straight and its width ranges from 1 to 24 millimeters. From an esoteric point of view, this line represents the Antakharana, the bridge of light that links us to our soul. The Faden carries strong regenerative energies through its cellular memory, since it has been injured and has healed itself many times throughout its development. Resonance with Faden Quartz gives us access to our own healing power, allowing it to be activated and reinforced by the quartz. The Faden Quartz is an interesting replica of the human being and its energetic potential. It makes the learning of different life lessons of incarnation easier.

Just like the Elestial, the Faden is linked to the angelic world and has the ability to act as a bridge between the angelic kingdom and the earth plane. In order to invoke protection, guidance, and the healing energies of angels, pure intentions are essential.

From a physical point of view, the Faden Quartz regenerates the nervous system and repairs lesions in the nerve tissues following the sectioning of a nerve. It helps one to recover from surgery, fractures, pulled muscles, and damaged blood vessels. It diminishes scars, reinforces the spine, and alleviates vertebral pain. The Faden Quartz is also an excellent protector when traveling by plane.

LASER QUARTZ

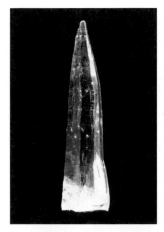

The Laser Quartz has just begun to resurface, at a time when humanity can begin to be trusted to explore a small portion of its potential. In meditation, it helps bridge the gap between the personality and the higher self. Laser Quartz are not necessarily beautiful in physical appearance, but this is their disguise, for they emit an incredibly high frequency of white light.

Lasers are very powerful as they contain the secret to laser-ray projection. Energy, or white light, moves through a laser at an extremely fast rate, with the potential to cut through metal. Tuning into a laser, one can gradually receive education in the advanced healing arts.

There is an enormous responsibility in owning and treating with a Laser Quartz. "Laser surgery" can be performed after one has undergone significant training, where old attachments and attitudes can literally be cut from the energetic field of an individual. It is important to keep in mind that one should never point a Laser Quartz directly at a person, for when a therapist projects their energy through it, it becomes a scalpel, and one can cut into the aura and cause holes and fissures.

A successful session can cut away habits of jealousy, anger, guilt, and even attachment to old partners or negative childhood events. This kind of treatment should only be done with the full permission and understanding of the client, and only after the person has really examined and processed their patterns, emotions, attachments, and attitudes. The individual must be honestly ready to let them go and replace them with more constructive attitudes; otherwise he or she will probably just return to their old ways. After a session, it is important to send the client home with some healing stones to place on the part of the body where the "surgery" was performed, usually the solar plexus or around the navel and hara. This will transmit soothing, healing energies and support the person during the transition.

LODOLITE QUARTZ

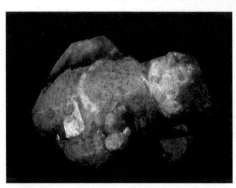

Lodolite Quartz is often called garden quartz, landscape quartz, or scenic quartz. In Greek, it means "stone from the mud." It can have multiple inclusions that resemble a magnificent coral reef. These colorful inclusions are presumed to be formed from a mixture of calcite, chlorite, and iron. Lodolite may be used as a decorative piece that can beautify and energize a room. It is also considered a formidable meditation companion, as Lodolite is said to stimulate the crown chakra and to communicate loving vibrations and energies of gentle strength. It is said to enhance communication with beings on the spiritual plane and heighten one's spiritual energies while ensuring that one stays grounded. Lodolite is further known for its therapeutic virtues and is particularly helpful in easing menstrual pain. It is known to emit strong curative energies when used in lithotherapy.

PHANTOM QUARTZ

The Phantom Quartz is so named due to the pyramidal inclusions found within it, often revealing a concrete aspect followed by a more subtle form. These pyramids can be a variety of colors, such as green formed by chlorite, and violet from amethyst. Just as the lifespan of a tree can be measured through its rings, a quartz may contain one or many pyramids signifying the different stages of its growth. Phantoms have experienced multiple phases of growth and contain many lifetimes of development while in the same form. They have the ability to carry us to our source and to reveal our original face. They can also help us to access our progression throughout our various lifetimes and to integrate experiences. Phantoms offer aid in building the bridge of light to our soul, which holds the potential to reveal truths about the true nature of our being. This process takes lifetimes, but Phantoms can help us throughout each successive step on the journey to Self.

QUARTZ CLUSTER

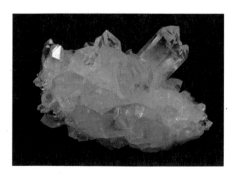

Clusters are several crystals living in harmony on a single matrix. They represent the advanced community, supporting each other by continuously transmitting energy to one another. They emit a strong and vibrant light while radiating a soothing, calming vibration. They can be placed in rooms where their capacity to calm discordant vibrations will melt away any friction and disharmony. They can also be placed between two people during meditation, or while engaging in creative conflict resolution. Group meetings seem to flow more easily with a cluster mediating in the center. Pictures of loved ones or those in need can be placed atop this quartz while directing positive thoughts and energies to them. Clusters are ideal to place other stones and small crystals on due to their superb cleansing and charging properties. They rarely need cleansing or charging themselves, but an occasional dusting and sunbath may be necessary at times, especially if they have been working hard.

SCEPTER QUARTZ

A Scepter is recognized as a crystal "head" that has been penetrated by a crystal "rod." In fact, it is a larger crystal that forms over an existing base. It actually resembles a scepter, as well as a phallus. It is said that the phallus point circulates and directs the energies of the quartz as a tool to enhance fertility. It is a symbol of power, as it harnesses the force of spirit expressed in nature. It presents us with an opportunity to learn the correct use of power. The energy of the Scepter tends to penetrate the heart chamber, stimulating the urge to create constructively.

The energy of Shiva, the Hindu god of destruction, imbibes these crystals, for establishing new and dynamic projects in the physical realm sometimes requires that old and outdated structures be broken down.

Scepters emit a high level of energy and have been used in therapeutic practices because of this fact. It is a crystal that gets to the heart of the matter, whether it is a physical disease or an emotional or mental imbalance. They emit an energy that penetrates and pierces, dissolving what doesn't work and then restructuring the energy to create harmony and balance.

SMOKY QUARTZ

Smoky Quartz has been naturally irradiated in the earth to produce a darkening effect inside a crystal. These crystals are natural warriors in that they are superb dissipaters of negative energies. They are quite familiar with the darkened aspects of this world of polarity, having themselves attained a certain mastery over it. They instinctively "descend" and penetrate the negative energy, where it is then neutralized. At the same time that destructive energies are dissolved, white light is injected, making these crystals highly effective tools for purification of the gross and subtle bodies.

They are also used as grounding crystals, helping those who have a tendency to have their head in the clouds. They are a great aid to those who have a difficult time facing reality and all of the demands and responsibilities that come with it. Carrying or consciously meditating with a programmed Smoky Quartz can help purify the causes of some self-destructive habits such as smoking and alcoholism. It can also help with some cases of depression and suicidal tendencies; all of these problems of course result from a strong urge to escape from the outer world and from painful feelings.

Keep in mind that these crystals are powerful, so it is important to start slow, perhaps with a lightly Smoky Quartz, and then move on to something darker. It may be wise to work conjointly with a healing stone such as a rose quartz or an amethyst, or even a citrine for joy, to help "digest" the process. If one works diligently with crystals, ardently seeking change and freedom from unhealthy patterns, a progressive and real transformation can occur. Smoky Quartz calls to our own inner warrior, challenging us to face what is no longer useful.

CRYSTAL OR QUARTZ

The words "crystal" and "quartz" are widely used in the nomenclature of the world of stones and crystals. Authors use them to describe crystalline processes.

Some people consider the word "crystal" to be more generic than the word "quartz," the latter designating more-specific formations such as "amethyst quartz." We note that quartz, made of crystal, is often called rock crystal or when we are talking about this type of quartz, as "amethyst quartz." In this book, it has been agreed to use the two names, which are both considered appropriate. You will thus find an alternation of "quartz" and "crystal," and both have the same meaning throughout this volume.

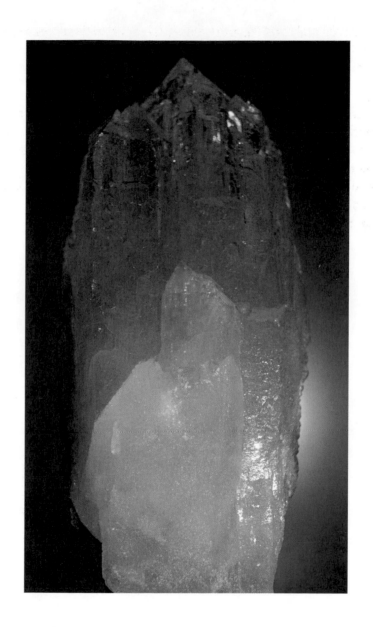

STONES, CRYSTALS AND THERAPEUTIC PROPERTIES

AGATE FAMILY

Crystal System: trigonal

Colors: blue, brown, yellow, red, green

Chakras: according to color

Hardness: 6.5 to 7

Origin: Brazil, India, Madagascar, Uruguay

Formation Process: magmatic

Chemical Composition: silicon oxide

Purification: cold water, salt water, incense, earth

Recharging: quartz cluster, sunlight

Generalities

In ancient times, agate was considered a lucky charm, a stone of protection. In India, Nepal, and Tibet, it is worn as an amulet and is still known for its virtues.

Lithotherapy

- Balances and harmonizes the body, mind, and spirit
- Cleans and stabilizes the aura, removing all negativity
- Stimulates and reinforces analytical abilities
- Reinforces powers of concentration and brings clarity of thought
- Revives inspiration and facilitates access to spiritual worlds
- Helps to discern the truth and to accept reality
- Gives strength and courage
- Stabilizes body energies
- Calms and balances both mother and child during pregnancy and labour
- Prevents the descent of the uterus and stimulates tissue regeneration of the uterus after childbirth
- Alleviates eye diseases (such as conjunctivitis)
- Treats gastritis and stomach tumors
- Reduces bladder and colon inflammation
- Facilitates digestion and excretion
- Reinforces blood vessels and tissues
- Eases skin ailments
- Purifies the lymphatic system and pancreas

Placed on the heart, agate treats emotional turmoil that prevents one from accepting love; placed on the stomach, it stimulates the digestion process.

BLUE LACE AGATE

Lithotherapy

· Activates and balances the throat chakra

· Encourages a positive attitude

· Neutralizes anger, infections, inflammations, and fever

· Calms the mind, encourages peace and tranquility, and elevates the consciousness

· Reduces inflammation and diminishes deformities caused by arthritis

· Fortifies the skeletal structure and treats broken bones

· Relieves irritated, red eyes and inflamed, irritated skin

· Treats shoulder and neck problems

· Alleviates thyroid and lymphatic deficiencies

· Calms throat infections

· Facilitates the functioning of the pancreas

FIRE AGATE

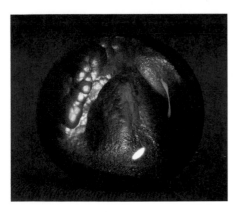

Lithotherapy

· Has an affinity with the root chakra

· Helps to ground oneself and to establish a connection of power with the earth

· Creates a shield around the body; represents a great protective force

- Incites to destroy and to transmute the "old"
- Helps eliminate obstacles to radical change
- Eliminates envy and destructive desire
- Calms fears and instills a profound feeling of security
- Revitalizes and energizes when exhausted
- Stimulates the libido
- Treats addiction and dependency
- Eases stomach problems
- Balances the endocrine and nervous systems
- Treats circulatory problems
- Fortifies night vision and clarifies inner vision
- Alleviates hot flashes and lowers body temperature

Moss Agate

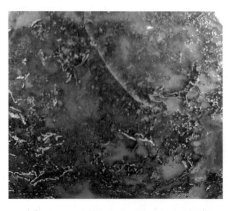

Chemical Composition: silicon oxide with chlorite

Lithotherapy

- Stabilizes and balances
- Awakens a love of nature
- Known as a stone of abundance, attracts wealth

- Alleviates pain during childbirth and favors easy delivery
- Speeds up recovery, especially after a long illness
- Used as an anti-inflammatory
- Purifies the circulatory system

- Facilitates lymphatic circulation
- Activates the immune system
- Prevents hypoglycemia
- Contributes to the production of phlegm, which prevents dry coughs, and reduces sensitivities to climatic conditions

ALEXANDRITE (VARIETY OF CHRYSOBERYL)

Crystal System: rhombic

Colors: violet in artificial light with emerald green reflections in the sunlight

Chakras: solar plexus, heart, third eye, crown

Hardness: 8.5

Origin: Brazil, Madagascar, Myanmar, Russia, Sri Lanka, Tasmania, United States, Zimbabwe

Formation Process: metamorphic

*

Chemical Composition: aluminum and glucinum oxide

Purification: salt water in low light, rinse in cold water, sunlight

Recharging: quartz cluster, sunlight

Generalities

Alexandrite was discovered in 1833 in the Ural Mountain Range that runs through western Russia. It was named in honor of Alexander II, czar of Russia. It became the national stone of Russia due its colors red and green, colors associated with the Russian army.

Lithotherapy

- Imparts balance between force and gentleness and between power and justice
- A stone of service or self-sacrifice for the good of others
- Clarifies dreams, inner images, and desires
- Facilitates strategic thought and planning
- Encourages risk-taking and listening to one's inner voice rather than depending solely on logic
- Stimulates the intuition, clairvoyance, and channeling
- Awakens willpower and a dynamic attitude, particularly when the task is challenging, stressful, or arduous
- Helps to cultivate intelligence and creativity
- Awakens the power to heal oneself
- Regenerates the liver
- Reduces inflammation
- Detoxifies
- Prevents heart problems and aneurisms
- Reduces cholesterol
- Improves blood circulation

AMAZONITE

Crystal System: triclinic

Color: blue-green

Chakras: all, but mainly heart and throat

Hardness: 6 to 6.5

Origin: Brazil, United States (Colorado), India, Russia, South Africa

Formation Process: magmatic, sedimentary, metamorphic

Chemical Composition: potassium aluminosilicate

Purification: cold water, incense, sunlight, earth

Recharging: quartz cluster, abundant sunlight

Generalities

According to legend, amazonite was the stone of the "Amazons," a group of female warriors who lived in a community without men.

Lithotherapy

· Helps to cultivate diplomatic communication

· Contributes to the development of intuition

· Facilitates self-expression

· Emits a strong soothing energy, which harmonizes the nervous system by dissipating worry, fear, and anger, and by balancing mood swings

· Encourages self-sufficiency and connection to one's inner power

· Strengthens weakened muscles

· Alleviates liver problems

- Encourages relaxation during childbirth, thus facilitating the opening of the cervix

- Fortifies nerves

- Balances thyroid and parathyroid glands

- Alleviates some brain ailments

- Harmonizes the pituitary gland and thymus as well as the neurovegetative system and internal organs

- Alleviates cardiac pain due to grief

- Resolves calcium deficiencies

- Has a beneficial influence on osteoporosis and tooth decay

- Soothes cramps and muscular spasms

Amazonite also protects against electromagnetic waves produced by microwave ovens and computers. For this purpose, it may be worn directly on one's person or set near the microwave oven or beside the computer. It is also possible to attach it to a cellular phone.

AMBER

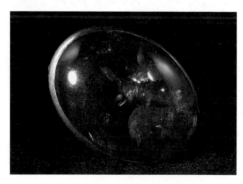

Crystal System: amorphous.

Colors: milky white, light yellow to brown, black, red, green tones, rarely blue

Chakras: throat, solar plexus

Hardness: 2 to 2.5

Origin: Canada, Dominican Republic, France, Myanmar, Romania

Formation Process: sedimentary

Chemical Composition: amorphous fossil resin, carbon based

Purification: quartz cluster, incense

Recharging: quartz cluster

Generalities

Although amber is actually resin, it is considered the first "precious stone" in the history of humanity. It has been used for more than 7,000 years for its therapeutic benefits; it has similar properties to penicillin.

Lithotherapy

· Possesses great wisdom

· Is the secret guardian of the earth

· Awakens inner memories

· Allows the body to balance and heal itself

· Provides a cheerful, gentle, and easy-going yet confident nature

· Encourages spontaneity, openness and respect

· Purifies the body, mind, and spirit

· Treats and regenerates the nervous system

· Balances the brain hemispheres

· Acts on stomach, spleen, and kidney disorders

· Relieves skin illnesses caused by liver disorder, accumulation of bile, and dysfunctional metabolism

· Helps with joint problems (such as formation of cartilage)

· Soothes acute dental pain in young children

Amber has powerful therapeutic properties. It acts effectively if worn often and over long periods of time. When treating infants and children with amber, it is recommended that the piece be worn by the mother in advance.

AMETHYST

Crystal System: trigonal

Colors: deep violet to pale lavender, almost to the point of being clear

Chakras: crown, third eye

Hardness: 7

Origin: Brazil, Canada, East Africa, Great Britain, India, Madagascar, Mexico, Russia, Siberia, Sri Lanka, United States, Uruguay

Formation Process: magmatic

Chemical Composition: silicon oxide, iron, manganese

Purification: salt water, cold water, incense, earth

Recharging: quartz cluster, sunlight (for short periods only or it may lose its luster)

Generalities

In ancient times, amethyst was known for its sobering effects and its ability to clear the mind. In the Middle Ages, it was recognized that this quartz instilled courage and banished negative thoughts, encouraging kindness and understanding.

Lithotherapy

- · Embodies the alchemical violet ray of transformation
- · Offers powerful protection
- · Brings clarity of mind
- · Increases clairvoyant vision
- · Aids visualization and clarifies dreams

- Stimulates inspiration and intuition
- Reinforces a sense of justice and proper discrimination
- Encourages honesty
- Calms an overactive inner dialogue
- Contributes to finding deep inner peace and to discovering inner wisdom
- Helps to overcome grief from mourning
- Eases addictions, such as to drugs or alcohol
- Calms passions, violent emotions, and anger
- Alleviates general pain and provides relaxation
- Help with diseases of the ectoderm of all organs
- Soothes nervous problems
- Calms the lungs and afflictions of the respiratory system
- Clears skin impurities (such as furuncle) and eases maladies of the skin and cases of swelling
- Soothes intestinal disorders and regularizes flora, even in the presence of parasites
- Reinforces the endocrine and immune systems
- Purifies the blood
- Activates the functioning of the right side of the brain and of the pituitary and pineal glands

Placed under a pillow, amethyst encourages deep sleep, alleviates nightmares, and allows for a clearer comprehension of dreams. For optimal results, it is best to wear amethyst on the body for a long period of time. For a particular ailment on a specific area of the body, such as an organ, it is recommended to place amethyst close to the affected area for an unlimited amount of time. It can also be placed directly on the chakra related to the problem for twenty minutes at a time.

AMETRINE

Crystal System: trigonal

Colors: yellow, violet

Chakras: solar plexus, third eye

Hardness: 7

Origin: Brazil, Bolivia, South America, Uruguay

Formation Process: magmatic

Chemical Composition: silicon oxide, iron, manganese

Purification: cold water, salt water, incense, sunlight, earth

Recharging: quartz cluster, sunlight

Generalities

Ametrine is a quartz with delimited zones of amethyst and citrine, bringing together characteristics and properties of both stones.

Lithotherapy

· Encourages confident and well-considered action

· Contributes to bringing together apparent opposites, for example, feminine and masculine energies

· Awakens optimism and arouses inner well-being

· Is recognized as a source of great creativity with powerful energy

· Encourages taking charge of one's life

· Facilitates acceptance of others, creating greater compatibility and cooperation in order to avoid passing judgment

· Raises the mind to higher levels of awareness

· Brings comprehension to the causes of chronic illnesses

· Protects during astral voyages

- Protects against physical dangers
- Eliminates stress and balances energies in the mind, allowing for better concentration during meditation
- Brings clarity of mind and better concentration
- Dissolves harmful emotional programming
- Sustains people suffering from chronic fatigue, depression, and problems linked to stress
- Releases blockages in the physical, emotional, and mental bodies
- Facilitates transformation
- Dissipates negativity in the aura
- Purifies the blood and revitalizes the body
- Purifies cellular metabolism and tissues
- Harmonizes interactions between internal organs
- Activates functions of the neurovegetative system
- Regenerates the physical body
- Reinforces the immune system

ANDALUSITE/CHIASTOLITE

Crystal System: rhombic

Colors: brown, gray (with a black cross), from green yellowish shades to green brown as a gem

Chakras: root, solar plexus

Hardness: 7.5

Origin: Brazil, Canada, Russia, Spain, United States

Formation Process: magmatic, metamorphic

Chemical Composition: aluminum silicate

Purification: cold water, salt water, incense, sunlight, earth (rarely necessary)

Recharging: quartz cluster, sunlight

Generalities

The name "Chiastolite" comes from the Greek word "chiastos," meaning "cruciform" or "form of an axis." The cross on the surface, made of two lines of the same length, is an ancient symbol for multiplication that comes from the actual sign of the arithmetic operation of the same name. Therefore, chiastolite symbolizes growth or multiplication. This ancient symbol, most commonly adopted by the Christian faith, holds many occult meanings. It is also known to have the power to neutralize curses and malevolent forces.

Lithotherapy

- Grants great protection
- Transforms chaos and conflict into harmony
- Contributes to the transition from one situation to another
- Neutralizes conditioning and programming
- Stabilizes emotions and helps one to remain centered
- Releases fears, particularly the fear of insanity, as well as guilt
- Soothes the nervous system
- Grounds and anchors to the physical plane
- Reinforces the intuition in order to achieve professional objectives
- Guides towards the expression of one's authentic self, aligned with one's life mission
- Fortifies analytical abilities
- Gives a sense of reality and objectivity, encouraging detachment
- Dissipates illusions
- Instills balance between the material world and our spiritual Selves
- Eases the transition at the time of death
- Encourages moderation in all things
- Instills balance and discrimination in acts of service and self-sacrifice
- Facilitates astral journeys, and the comprehension and exploration of immortality
- Alleviates hyperacidity, rheumatism, and gout
- Fortifies nerves during weakened states, diminished cognitive capacities, and reduced mobility
- Treats the shoulders
- Balances the immune system

GREEN ANDALUSITE

Lithotherapy

· Provides balance

· Purifies the heart

· Releases emotional hang-ups, particularly those caused by anger and old emotional traumas

· Used in psychotherapy sessions

*

ANGEL AURA QUARTZ

Crystal System: trigonal

Color: pink, yellow, and blue iridescent reflections in a clear crystal

Chakras: crown, superior chakras up to the crown

Hardness: 7

Origin: quartz modified by humans

Formation Process: magmatic

Chemical Composition: silicon oxide with silver and platinum

Purification: cold water, salt water, incense, sunlight, earth

Recharging: quartz cluster, sunlight

Generalities

This crystal has been irradiated with a fine dust of silver, platinum, and other metals, which give off colorful reflections reminiscent of angel wings. Its fiery aura inspires the name "angel aura quartz."

Lithotherapy

· Has an energetic connection to the angelic kingdom

· Inspires the possibility to communicate with spiritual beings, angels, and divinities

· Allows access to our "inner temple," a place of rest and purification

· Creates an atmosphere of tranquillity and a sense of satisfaction

· Encourages unity with the beauty present everywhere, as much in nature as within ourselves

· Purifies the chakras and the aura

· Activates the light on physical and subtle levels; brings joy, light, and optimism

· Helps eliminate programmed beliefs and erroneous mental attitudes

· Protects from people who tend to deplete energy

· Offers the possibility to activate and integrate the "rainbow" body

· Deepens meditation

· Contributes to integrating new knowledge acquired in meditation

· Inspires one to go beyond illusions

· Instills force and courage into those who truthfully desire to reach realization

Apatite Family

Green apatite on calcite

Crystal System: hexagonal

Colors: white, blue, brown, gray, yellow, crimson, dark red, green, violet

Chakras: heart, throat, third eye

Hardness: 5

Origin: Brazil, India, Madagascar, Myanmar, United States

Formation Process: magmatic, metamorphic, sedimentary

Chemical Composition: calcium phosphate with fluorine and chlorine

Purification: cold water, incense, sunlight, earth

Recharging: quartz cluster, sunlight

Generalities

Apatite is a generally massive and opaque phosphate, rarely transparent and crystalline. In the past, this stone was easily confused with other minerals such as beryl or calcite. In 1786, it received the name of "apatao" from the Greek word for "mislead."

Used with other stones, apatite allows for easy achievement of an expected result. It must be worn directly on the body, around the area in need.

Lithotherapy

- Allows for the opening of the consciousness and facilitates inner contact
- Deepens meditation
- Arouses inspiration toward humanitarian aid
- Fights against apathy

- Vivifies and acts against exhaustion, especially when overindulging in activities

- Enhances motivation and helps to mobilize energy reserves

- Overcomes emotional exhaustion

- Reduces irritability and aggressive tendencies

- Favors communication and self-expression on all levels

- Helps to overcome grief, anger, and inertia

- Stimulates creativity and intellect

- Balances physical, mental, emotional, and spiritual bodies as well as the chakras

- Facilitates cellular regeneration as well as cartilage formation in bones and teeth (helps with rickets, arthritis, problems of the joints, broken bones)

- Contributes to better calcium absorption

- Calms hyperactivity and stimulates when overly inert

BLUE APATITE

Lithotherapy

- Favors contact with higher spiritual planes

- Facilitates public speaking

- Intensifies group communication

- Activates the throat chakra

- Soothes heartache and emotional troubles

Yellow Apatite

*

Lithotherapy

· Helps to eliminate toxins

· Activates the solar plexus

· Extracts stagnant energy, easing apathy and depression

· Increases concentration

· Relieves digestive problems

· Eliminates cellulite

· Treats the liver, pancreas, gallbladder, and spleen

· Reduces the appetite when taken as an elixir

Apophyllite

Crystal System: quadratic

Colors: white, yellowish, clear, blue green

Chakras: heart, crown, third eye

Hardness: 4.5 to 5

Origin: Australia, Brazil, Czech Republic, Great Britain, India, Italy, Norway

Formation Process: magmatic

Chemical Composition: complex calcaro-potassic silicate with fluorine

Purification: cold water, incense, sunlight, earth

Recharging: quartz cluster, sunlight

Generalities

Apophyllite is a stone rich in water, which confers a superior energetic conductivity than other phyllosilicates. A highly spiritual stone, it allows us to reach a deeper state of relaxation and receptivity.

Placed on the throat, apophyllite soothes asthma attacks; it soothes the eyes when placed directly on them.

Lithotherapy

· Favors an examination of one's own behavior

· Encourages the discovery of one's true Self

· Known as the "Stone of Truth," it encourages honesty

· Facilitates remaining true to oneself at all times

· Instills tranquility and calm

· Alleviates fears and oppressive feelings

· Releases repressed emotions

· Incites us to overcome problems and insecurities

· Brings light to difficult times

· Helps to release fixations and rigid thought patterns

· Encourages feeling at ease in one's body

· Soothes respiratory problems

· Favors regeneration of the skin and mucous membranes

· Neutralizes allergies

Aqua Aura Quartz

Crystal System: trigonal

Color: blue, from pale to dark

Chakras: throat, third eye

Hardness: 7

Origin: Brazil, Madagascar, United States (Arkansas)

Formation Process: magmatic

Chemical Composition: silicon with gold

Purification: cold water, salt water, incense, sunlight, earth

Recharging: quartz cluster, sunlight

Generalities

The aqua aura is a quartz that has gone through a laboratory process of radiation with pure gold. The result is a radiant blue quartz with rainbow reflections.

Lithotherapy

· Purifies the aura

· Stimulates the throat chakra

· Encourages sincere communication

· Calms and balances the emotional body

· Attenuates aggressiveness and feverishness, and releases stress

· Activates all the chakras

· Reinforces the curative properties of other stones

· Protects against psychic and psychological attacks and negative intrusions

· Activates the third eye, bringing concentration and clarity of mind

· Helps develop clairvoyance and clairaudience

· Reinforces and supports the thymus and immune system

AQUAMARINE

Crystal System: hexagonal

Colors: green to clear blue

Chakras: crown, throat, third eye

Hardness: 7.5 to 8

Origin: Brazil, India, Madagascar, Myanmar, United States

Formation Process: magmatic

Chemical Composition: aluminum and beryllium silicate

Purification: cold water, salt water, incense, sunlight, earth

Recharging: quartz cluster, sunlight

Generalities

Legend states that aquamarine changes color as a way of helping its owner distinguish true from false and friend from enemy. Ancient civilizations used it to confer well-being, stimulate memory, and awaken clairvoyant abilities. It is also said that sailors wore it for protection against drowning.

Lithotherapy

· Stimulates, activates, and purifies the throat chakra

· Opens communication with higher planes and dimensions

· Supports meditation practices

- Incites one to speak the truth and to release emotions
- Diminishes stress
- Calms and clears the mind
- Stimulates spiritual development
- Opens one up to a larger vision
- Arouses clairvoyance and mediumistic abilities
- Encourages one to be frank, straightforward, dynamic, and perseverant
- Incites tolerance, encouraging one to avoid making judgments
- Alleviates fears, anxiety, and morose thoughts
- Awakens the will to achieve goals and leads one to success
- Harmonizes the pituitary and thyroid glands, regularizing growth and hormonal imbalance
- Treats sore throat
- Improves eyesight in the case of myopia (nearsightedness) or farsightedness
- Alleviates excessive reaction of the immune system and allergies

Aquamarine can be worn at all times in contact with the skin. In the case of eyesight problems, place it directly on closed eyes

ARAGONITE

Crystal System: rhombic

Colors: white, blue, yellow, golden yellow, brownish red, green, greenish brown

Chakras: according to color

Hardness: 3.5 to 4

Origin: Great Britain, Namibia, Spain

Formation Process: magmatic, sedimentary

Chemical Composition: calcium carbonate

Purification: cold water, incense, abundant sunlight

Recharging: quartz cluster, sunlight

Generalities

Aragonite is a stone that anchors us to the earth and reinforces our connection with Mother Earth. It accompanies us into the past, helping to resolve conflicts and issues that keep us from moving forward.

Lithotherapy

- Increases vibrations and anchors one to the physical body in meditation
- Stabilizes and balances
- Alleviates stress and banishes anger
- Stimulates communication on higher planes of consciousness
- Teaches patience and tolerance
- Helps to maintain a state of well-being and acceptance during periods of great responsibility
- Awakens powers of discrimination for those who give too much of themselves
- Teaches one to delegate when necessary
- Favors reliability
- Keeps one practical and grounded
- Encourages one to feel at ease in one's body
- Helps to warm extremities
- Alleviates vitamin A and D deficiencies
- Helps prevent hair loss, wrinkles, and callused feet

Aventurine

Crystal System: trigonal

Color: green

Chakra: heart

Hardness: 7

Origin: Brazil, India, Russia

Formation Process: magmatic, metamorphic, sedimentary

Chemical Composition: silicate oxide

Purification: cold water, salt water, incense, sunlight, earth

Recharging: quartz cluster, sunlight

Generalities

The name "aventurine" comes from the term "a ventura" in Italian, which means "by chance."

Lithotherapy

· Benefits the heart chakra

· Brings comfort and balance and calms emotional stress, especially when combined with rose quartz

· Arouses deep relaxation and great satisfaction

· Fulfills those who do not feel loved or who find it difficult to open their hearts

· Strengthens leadership qualities

· Favors empathy and compassion

· Inculcates perseverance

· Stimulates creativity

- Balances masculine and feminine energies
- Alleviates stuttering and severe neurosis
- Encourages tolerance towards others
- Grants courage to live one's truth from the heart
- Reinforces, stabilizes and regenerates the heart
- Treats skin diseases caused by nervous tension
- Relieves insomnia
- Exercises a beneficial influence on the thymus, conjunctive tissue, and nervous system
- Regularizes growth from birth to age seven
- Balances the blood pressure and stimulates metabolism
- Reduces cholesterol and helps prevent arteriosclerosis and heart attacks
- Produces an anti-inflammatory effect in cases of skin rashes, allergies, migraines, and eye inflammation
- Soothes pain
- Calms nausea
- Supports the adrenal glands and the urogenital and muscular systems
- Treats the lungs, throat, and sinuses
- Creates a network of connections protecting against geopathic stress around gardens and homes
- Absorbs electromagnetic fog and protects against environmental pollution (protects from electromagnetic emissions when attached to cellular phone)
- Supports during the treatment of malignant diseases

Aventurine can be worn as a pendant or a necklace, held in the hand for a certain period, or in some acute cases, placed on the region to be treated.

AZEZTULITE

Crystal System: hexagonal

Colors: translucent or white

Chakras: all, but mainly third eye and crown

Hardness: 7

Origin: United States (North Carolina)

Formation Process: unknown

Chemical Composition: unknown

Purification: none necessary

Recharging: none necessary

Generalities

Considered to be a "Stone of the New Age," azeztulite has one of the purest and highest vibrations in the mineral kingdom.

Lithotherapy

- Elevates vibrations to favor spiritual evolution
- Stimulates expansion of consciousness
- Facilitates meditation
- Guides one to a state of "no mind"
- Creates a spiral of protection around the physical body
- Generates vision and inspiration
- Opens the third-eye and crown chakras
- Helps to obtain guidance from the future in order to make important decisions
- Beneficial in cases of cancer and cellular disorders

· Reactivates and reawakens perseverance and motivation in those suffering from chronic illness

AZURITE

Crystal System: monoclinic

Color: deep blue

Chakras: throat, third eye

Hardness: 3.5 to 4

Origin: Australia, Brazil, Czech Republic, France, Norway, Russia, United States

Formation Process: sedimentary

Chemical Composition: basic copper carbonate

Purification: cold water, incense, moonlight

Recharging: quartz cluster, moonlight, limited amount of sunlight

Generalities

Known as the "Stone of Heaven," azurite was considered a sacred stone to the First Nations people, who believed that it would facilitate contact with spiritual guides.

Lithotherapy

· Activates the throat and third-eye chakras

· Brings comfort and balance

· A powerful accelerator that brings great aid to the process of transformation

· Facilitates deep meditation

- Encourages confrontation with the reality of oneself, piercing illusions and delusions

- Accentuates clarity of mind, creativity, inspiration, and intuition

- Provides soothing effects to a restless mind

- Facilitates out-of-body experiences, stimulating the consciousness, and elevating it to a higher plane

- Motivates and guides one to face and overcome fears

- Represents the will to know and the will to change

- Reveals and liberates from imprints of the past

- Helps to reveal reasons for psychosomatic illnesses

- Activates and purifies the liver and gallbladder

- Aids cerebral and nerve activity

- Stimulates the thyroid gland and consequently growth

- Treats throat and spinal cord problems

AZURITE-MALACHITE

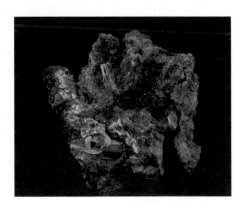

Lithotherapy

- Neutralizes negativity and harmonizes, thereby awakening an interest for everything and everyone that surround us

- Activates openness to oneself and others

- Encourages willingness to serve

- Reduces anxiety and instills feelings of well-being

- Supports in times of pain and misfortune, helping to free repressed emotions, to listen to one's heart, and to express innermost feelings

- Vivifies, detoxifies, defuses, and supports the immune system

· Helps to suppress tumors

· Alleviates joint problems (such as arthritis and arthrosis) and reduces joint inflammation

· Acts against cardiac diseases and asthma

Azurite with malachite can be held in the hands or placed on the third eye during meditation and contemplation. It is best for this stone to have direct contact with the skin, on or around the area affected, as it will directly absorb the energies causing the problem (such as hematoma, fractured bones, rheumatism, or internal pain).

BERYL FAMILY

Crystal System: hexagonal

Colors: yellow, yellow to blue-green (heliodore), gold (golden beryl), red (bixbite), transparent (goshenite), green

Chakras: from the root to the crown according to colors

Hardness: 7.5 to 8

Origin: Brazil, Madagascar, Pakistan, South Africa, Ural Mountains

Formation Process: magmatic

Chemical Composition: aluminium and beryllium silicate with cesium

Purification: cold water, salt water, incense, sunlight, earth (rarely necessary)

Recharging: quartz cluster, regular sunlight

Generalities

Transparent beryl is pure, with no foreign minerals altering its composition. Colored beryl contains other minerals that grant it its particular color. For example, iron will tint it yellow, gold, and sometimes blue, while lithium and manganese will tint it red.

In the past, beryl was known for its detoxifying power and for its positive effects on the eyesight. The German word for glasses, "brille," comes from the word "beryl."

Lithotherapy

· Encourages determination, efficiency, multitasking, and vision

· Shows how to accomplish what is necessary to meet ends

· Helps with stress management

· Allows to actualize one's potential

· Fortifies courage

· Encourages positive thinking

· Discourages overanalysis and anxiety

· Instills initiative and independence

· Vivifies the will toward success

· Stimulates the elimination organs

· Fortifies the pulmonary and circulatory systems

· Enhances resistance to toxins and pollutants

· Treats the liver, heart, and stomach

· Benefits the spine and treats concussions

· Alleviates throat infections when taken as an elixir

BLUE BERYL

*

Lithotherapy

· Treats shortsightedness and farsightedness

GOLD BERYL

Lithotherapy

· Teaches initiative and independence

· Calms nervousness and excessive emotions due to stress or overwork

· Stimulates the crown and solar plexus chakras

Pink Beryl (Morganite)

Lithotherapy

- Draws and maintains love

- Encourages gentle thoughts and actions

- Creates space, allowing one to make the most out of life

- Provides beneficial effects on the nervous system

- Maintains stability in the emotional body during change and transition

- Oxygenates and reorganizes cells, which is beneficial against tuberculosis, asthma, emphysema, cardiac problems, dizzy spells, impotence, and lung blockages

Red Beryl (Bixbite)

Lithotherapy

- Energizes

- Charges and clears the root chakra

BLOODSTONE (HELIOTROPE)

Crystal System: trigonal

Color: green, red

Chakras: root, heart

Hardness: 6.5 to 7

Origin: Australia, Brazil, China, Czech Republic, India, Russia, United States

Formation Process: sedimentary

Chemical Composition: iron oxide

Purification: distilled salt water, cold water, incense, sunlight, earth

Recharging: quartz cluster, sunlight

Generalities

In the Middle Ages, the red stain on the stone was believed to be a trace of the blood of Christ; it was said that the stone possessed special magical powers.

Lithotherapy

- Known as the stone of the spiritual warrior
- Increases intuition and creativity
- Repels evil and negative influences
- Stimulates dreams
- Anchors high energies into the body
- Confers courage, force, and determination to confront all the challenges of terrestrial life
- Urges one to act in the present moment
- Brings the recognition that chaos precedes transformation

- Encourages "noble sacrifice," self-effacement, and idealism
- Awakens the most noble altruistic characteristics
- Calms the mind and dispels confusion
- Facilitates decision making
- Helps to adjust to unusual situations
- Anchors heart energy
- Reduces irritation, aggressiveness, and impatience
- Invites spirituality into everyday life
- Carries energy into the body and mind in the case of exhaustion
- A great purifier, it stimulates immunity at times of acute infection
- Activates the circulation of the lymphatic system and the entire metabolism
- Detoxifies the liver, intestines, kidneys, spleen, and gallbladder
- Purifies the blood
- Regularizes and supports blood circulation as well as blood-filled organs

Boji Stones

Crystal System: cubic

Colors: brown to black

Chakras: throat, third eye, root

Hardness: 7.5

Origin: United States

Formation Process: sedimentary

Chemical Composition: Some authors describe them as fossils; others claim they contain pyrite

Purification: incense, earth

Recharging: quartz cluster, limited sunlight

Generalities

Boji stones can disintegrate if left on the ground or in the open air. Although they come as a pair, they should always be kept apart, as regular contact will also cause them to eventually disintegrate. The energy of the smooth stone is feminine while that of the rougher stone is masculine.

Lithotherapy

- Grounds and protects
- Supports people who feel uncomfortable in their present incarnation
- Favors a smooth return to the earth plane and within the body
- Helps to overcome obsessions and patterns by making them more evident
- Balances and harmonizes masculine and feminine energies
- Increases energy and aligns the chakras and subtle bodies
- Releases repressed emotions and heals painful memories
- Stimulates and regularizes the circulation of energy throughout the meridians
- Relieves pain and favors tissue regeneration
- Repairs auric holes and replenishes lost energy
- Helps to confront the darker side of the personality
- Has a preventive effect against disease in general
- Less suitable to relieve very acute pain

A pair of Boji stones can be held in the hands for ten to thirty minutes; test which hand feels best with either the masculine or feminine stone. They can also be placed near the area on the body to be treated. One can be placed at the head and the other at the feet for a balancing, energizing, and grounding effect.

BULL'S EYE OR OX EYE

Crystal System: trigonal

Colors: shimmering nuances of red and reddish brown

Chakras: solar plexus, root

Hardness: 7

Origin: Australia, Brazil

Formation Process: sedimentary

Chemical Composition: silicon oxide

Purification: quartz cluster, cold water, salt water, incense, sunlight, earth

Recharging: quartz cluster, sunlight

Generalities

The bull's eye is actually red tiger eye with a red or chestnut brown predominance. Just as good a protector as the tiger eye, it is, however, more aggressive and specifically employed to obtain strength and courage.

Lithotherapy

· Brings suppleness to the human psyche

· Encourages setting goals for oneself, and to persevere without dispersing energy

· Energizes and clears the root chakra, grounding one to the physical plane

· Allows for regulation and balance of earth energies into the root chakra

· A great protector, it repels negative energies from the auric field and sends them back to their source

· Wards off unnecessary obstacles in daily life

- Protects against theft of material goods
- Stimulates the survival instinct
- Supports in business affairs and projects
- A stone for physical suppleness, it is useful for any problem related to the back
- Brings warmth, force, and physical dynamism
- Reinforces the whole body structure from the base of the spine and is therefore particularly recommended for athletes
- Gives the necessary energy to sustain physical effort until the goal is reached

CALCITE FAMILY

Crystal System: trigonal

Colors: almost all colors

Chakras: according to color

Hardness: 3

Origin: found throughout the world.

Formation Process: magmatic, sedimentary

Chemical Composition: calcium carbonate with iron or manganese (also traces of cobalt, lead, and strontium depending on color)

Purification: cold water, incense, sunlight, earth

Recharging: quartz cluster, sunlight

Green calcite

Generalities

Calcite was formerly used in the form of lime to treat skin problems, tumors, warts, and infectious wounds.

Lithotherapy

- Balances emotions and stabilizes feminine and masculine polarities
- Calms fears, reduces stress, and quietens the mind
- Provides stability, self-confidence, and constancy
- Acts against laziness and stimulates the ability to excel
- Encourages efficiency and swift action
- Improves judgment and reinforces memory
- Calms excessive energy
- Repels negative energies and intensifies personal energy
- Treats the kidneys, pancreas, and gallbladder
- Stimulates immunity and encourages growth in children
- Treats skin ailments
- Relieves intestinal problems
- Encourages coagulation and favors regeneration of tissues and bones
- Normalizes the heartbeat and fortifies the heart
- Purifies the elimination organs
- Aids with proper functioning of the pancreas and gallbladder
- Favors absorption of calcium in the bones while destroying calcifications and fortifying the skeletal system and joints

Calcite is a powerful purifier and potent amplifier with the ability to swiftly increase one's vital energy. Calcite can be held in the hand or placed on the body, on or around the distressed area. It can also be placed on the respective chakra for twenty minutes at a time, according to its color.

BLACK CALCITE

*

Lithotherapy

· Stimulates recall of past memories for the purpose of healing and letting go

· Grounds the energy body to the physical body following trauma or great stress

· Alleviates depression

· A useful companion during existential crises and profound transitions and changes

BLUE CALCITE

Lithotherapy

· Has an affinity with the throat chakra

· Favors clear communication

· Soothes the throat and lungs and reduces thyroid inflammation

· Reduces stress and anxiety

· Encourages recuperation and relaxation

· Supports one during channeling

· Absorbs negative energy, filters it, and returns it to the transmitter

· Regulates blood pressure

Clear Calcite

Lithotherapy

· Refines and aligns all chakras

· Provides deep soul healing

· Revitalizes the subtle bodies

· Improves and sharpens inner and outer vision

· Powerfully purifies and disinfects

Gold or Yellow Calcite

Lithotherapy

· Generally placed at the crown chakra and the solar plexus

· Stimulates willpower

· Raises the spirits

· Intensifies meditation, inducing a profound state of relaxation

· Emits a very expansive energy that encourages mental agility by anchoring superior mental energies within the physical form

· Purifies the elimination organs

GREEN CALCITE

Lithotherapy

- Beneficial to the heart chakra
- Dissipates rigid beliefs and patterns
- Helps to release attachments to what may seem familiar and comfortable, yet actually stagnating and useless
- Calms distress caused by anger
- Stimulates the thymus
- Reinforces the immune system
- Relieves bacterial infections
- Alleviates arthritis and muscle and ligament strain
- Soothes fevers, burns, and inflammations
- Supports the adrenal glands
- Restores balance to the nervous system
- Reduces stress and calms heart palpitations
- Reinforces the heart and regulates its rhythm

Green calcite is highly absorbent and purifying and therefore requires more vigilant care and cleaning.

OPTICAL CALCITE

Lithotherapy

· Amplifies images and soothes eye problems

· Helps one to understand the double meaning of words

· Diminishes tension-causing migraines

· Purifies the subtle bodies

ORANGE CALCITE

Lithotherapy

· Vibrates with the solar plexus due to its warm and welcoming energy

· Purifies and treats the hara

· Balances emotions

· Dissipates fear

· Alleviates depression, helping one to maximize one's full potential

· Treats problems related to the reproductive system

· Stimulates the libido

· Supports the gallbladder and purifies the kidneys

· Eases intestinal problems such as constipation, diarrhea and irritable bowel syndrome

· Eliminates mucus

PINK CALCITE

Lithotherapy

· Known as the "stone of the heart" that works closely with the kingdom of devas

· A "stone of forgiveness," it frees one from that which imprisons the heart, such as fear and sorrow

· Favors inner awareness

· Encourages self-acceptance

· Treats nervous problems, eliminating tension and anxiety

· Prevents nightmares

· Dissolves resistance

· Supports those who suffer from trauma

RED CALCITE

Lithotherapy

· Vibrates well with the root and heart chakras

· Increases energy, raises spirits and augments willpower

· Transmits a love of life

· Eliminates stagnant energy

· Eases lower back and sciatic nerve* pain as well as hip, leg, and knee problems

· Relieves constipation

· Treats the reproductive system

· Purifies and stimulates the genitals

· Treats infertility

CARNELIAN

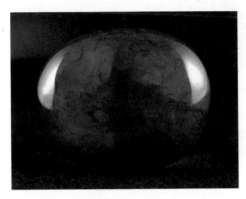

Crystal System: trigonal

Color: orange, red, brownish orange, brownish red

Chakras: hara, root

Hardness: 6.5 to 7

Origin: Brazil, Czech Republic, Egypt, England, India, Peru, Romania, Uruguay

Formation Process: magmatic

Chemical Composition: silicon and iron oxide

Purification: cold water, salt water, incense, sunlight, earth

Recharging: quartz cluster, abundant sunlight

Generalities

Carnelian has evolved with the terrestrial cycle and has become one of the power stones of the Aquarian age. It communicates a message of love and symbolizes the force and beauty of our planet.

Lithotherapy

· A stone of courage, it instills self-confidence and encourages standing up for oneself

· Banishes negative emotions such as fear, rage, envy, jealousy and resentment

· Alleviates depression and awakens inner joy

· Energizes and rejuvenates

· Stimulates the mind and clears mental confusion

· Favors concentration and constructive problem solving

- Restores trust and communicates love following abuse and trauma
- Aligns the etheric with the physical body
- Facilitates connection with the higher self
- Enhances fertility
- Helps to clear physico-energetic blockages in reproductive organs that cause sterility and impotence
- Stimulates the libido and creativity
- Activates the assimilation of vitamins, nutrients, and mineral salts in the small intestines
- Improves the quality of blood and stops hemorrhaging
- Ensures the proper elimination of toxins from the organs and tissues
- Relieves lower back problems, rheumatism, arthritis and neuralgia
- Contributes to the proper functioning of the digestive system including the liver, gallbladder and pancreas
- Benefits the bladder

Carnelian attracts abundance and acts as a guardian against unwanted energies and visitors when placed near the entrance of a home. In the past, it was used to protect the dead during their journey into the next life. It may be worn as jewelry or placed directly on the skin as needed.

CAT'S EYE (CYMOPHANE)

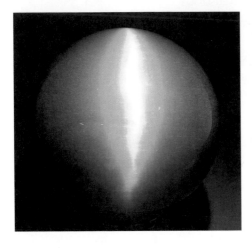

Crystal System: trigonal

Colors: brownish green to yellow with a light iridescent stripe on the surface that moves according to the direction of light

Chakras: heart, solar plexus

Hardness: 8.5

Origin: Brazil, China

Formation Process: magmatic, metamorphic

Chemical Composition: beryllium aluminate

Purification: cold water, salt water, incense, moonlight, sunlight, earth

Recharging: quartz cluster, moonlight, sunlight

Lithotherapy

· Helps find solutions to apparently unsolvable problems

· Attracts good fortune

· Offers protection against negative energies

· Contributes to freeing oneself from harmful behaviors

· Awakens courage

· Favors creativity

· Calms impulsiveness

· Elevates the spirits and communicates joy

· Inspires forgiveness

· Encourages flexibility, versatility, and adaptability

· Leads to professional, financial, and emotional success

· Calms stress

- Encourages philosophical reflection
- Supports athletes who must make short but intense efforts (such as sprints and jumps)
- Confers energy, suppleness, and audacity
- Increases precision and speed in body reflexes and movements
- Alleviates hearing problems
- Facilitates night vision
- Regulates and protects the liver, gallbladder, pancreas, and bowels
- Relieves the bronchial tubes and lungs and treats asthma
- Assists the body when low in minerals and vitamins
- Supports the central nervous system
- Eliminates toxins

Celestite

Crystal System: rhombic

Colors: blue, red, reddish brown, yellow, white

Chakras: heart, throat

Hardness: 3 to 3.5

Origin: Egypt, Great Britain, Lebanon, Madagascar, Mexico, Peru

Formation Process: sedimentary

Chemical Composition: strontium sulfate

Purification: cold water, incense

Recharging: quartz cluster, sunlight

Generalities

Known as an exceptional stone, celestite dissolves pain and instills love. Bearer of the energy of maternal love, this stone provides great support for children.

Lithotherapy

- Encourages spiritual growth
- Stimulates clairvoyance, dream recall, and contact with the angelic realm
- Cultivates purity of heart
- Balances yin and yang energies
- Helps to maintain an atmosphere of harmony during stressful times
- Improves difficult relationships through negotiation
- Increases artistic creativity
- Favors deep peace, allowing one to open up to new experiences
- Teaches one to trust in Divine Wisdom
- Soothes fiery emotions
- Sustains clear ideas and flowing communication
- Radiates maternal love

CHALCEDONY FAMILY

Crystal System: trigonal

Colors: great variety of colors

Chakras: according to color

Hardness: 6.5 to 7

Origin: Austria, Brazil, Czech Republic, Great Britain, India, Madagascar, Mexico, Morocco, New Zealand, Norway, Russia, Slovakia, United States

Formation Process: magmatic, sedimentary

Chemical Composition: silicon oxide

Blue chalcedony

Purification: cold water; salt water to be used in moderation, as chalcedony is a porous stone; incense; sunlight; earth

Recharging: quartz cluster, sunlight

Generalities

In past civilizations, chalcedony was associated with air and water elements and was therefore used to influence atmospheric conditions. It was also used to heal ailments caused by weather conditions, such as cold temperatures. Chalcedony was sculpted into drinking bowls as an antidote to poisonous liquids.

Lithotherapy

· Instills a sense of belonging to a group

· Increases goodwill toward others

· Supports during telepathic communication

· Prevents nightmares and negative thoughts and emotions

- Absorbs negative energies and suppresses them in order to prevent propagation
- Encourages kindness and generosity
- Diminishes hostile feelings and doubt toward oneself
- Encourages inner reflection
- Harmonizes the physical, emotional, and mental body with the spiritual self
- Transforms melancholy into joy and enthusiasm
- Purifies open wounds
- Helps to develop maternal instinct and activate milk production in the mammary glands
- Encourages mineral assimilation while preventing deposits in the veins
- Increases physical energy
- Soothes the eyes
- Treats the gallbladder and spleen
- Supports the blood and the circulatory system

BLUE CHALCEDONY

Lithotherapy

- Encourages the ability to listen and understand others and to express oneself correctly
- Incites understanding and appreciation of life from all kingdoms, that is, human, animal, plant, and mineral
- Stimulates telepathy and communication with invisible worlds
- Useful for therapists as it encourages the healthy awareness of subconscious truths that are difficult to access
- Helps to accept new situations without feeling lost

- Activates the memory, eliminates stress, and increases efficiency (ideal for students)
- Stimulates the throat and third-eye chakras
- Excels in supporting diplomats and orators
- Stimulates awareness of one's feelings, desires, and needs
- Calms the emotional body and the mind
- Reduces anxiety and relieves panic attacks
- Dissolves feelings of despair and replaces them with optimism
- Reinforces vocal organs and prevents irritation
- Treats throat problems and infections
- Helps to overcome difficulties of the respiratory system
- Alleviates harmful consequences caused by tobacco
- Acts as an anti-inflammatory
- Lowers blood pressure
- Ensures good circulation of organic fluids (such as lymph and blood)
- Treats edema
- Fortifies the immune system
- Regularizes production of insulin and is therefore useful in early stages of diabetes
- Contributes to the balanced secretion of the endocrine glands

DENDRITIC CHALCEDONY

Lithotherapy

· Helps to differentiate real objectives from opinion or influence of others

· Releases the mind from unconscious habits and memories from the past

· Clarifies confused thoughts

· Invites calm during stressful times

· Favors tolerant interaction without judgment

*

· Encourages living in the present moment and grants the courage to face unpleasant situations

· Supports one during chronic illness

· Diminishes effects of nicotine addiction

· Increases assimilation of copper in the body

· Treats the liver

· Diminishes inflammation of female sexual organs

PINK CHALCEDONY

Lithotherapy

· Inspires kindness, empathy, and cordiality

· Encourages active listening and understanding in order to help others overcome difficulties

· Instills inner peace and profound trust

· Favors curiosity and childlike wonder

*

· Awakens the desire to always learn more

· Supports in the art of storytelling

· Fortifies the heart and immune system

· Activates lymphatic circulation

· Treats psychosomatic diseases

RED CHALCEDONY

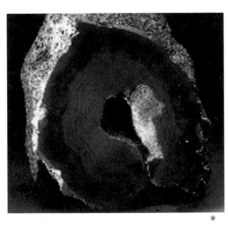

Lithotherapy

· Confers vigor and necessary persistence to reach goals

· Incites wisdom and discrimination as to when it is the time to fight and when it is necessary to give in

· Favors an open mind

· Reinforces motivation and trust

*

101

- Suppresses hunger
- Stimulates blood coagulation and circulation without increasing blood pressure

If overused, red chalcedony may inhibit nutrient absorption within the intestines and may cause nausea; it is therefore recommended to use it for short periods of time.

CHALCOPYRITE

Crystal System: quadratic

Colors: golden metallic sheen, sometimes with orange nuances and multicolored iridescence on the surface

Chakras: crown, third eye

Hardness: 3.5 to 4

Origin: South Africa, Spain, United States

Formation Process: magmatic, metamorphic, sedimentary

Chemical Composition: copper and iron sulfate

Purification: cold water, incense, sunlight, earth

Recharging: quartz cluster, abundant sunlight

Generalities

Chalcopyrite is a stone that is dynamic and stimulating for the mind and in harmony with spiritual energies.

Lithotherapy

- Powerful general disinfectant
- Soothes rheumatism
- Alleviates hepatic or abdominal pains
- Improves blood irrigation

CHAROITE

Crystal System: monoclinic

Colors: violet purple scattered with white and deep violet

Chakra: third eye

Hardness: 5 to 6

Origin: Russia

Formation Process: metamorphic

Chemical Composition: hydrated potassium, sodium, and calcium silicate

Purification: cold water, incense, moonlight, earth

Recharging: quartz cluster, moonlight

Generalities

This new stone manifests itself when the human race needs its energy. Charoite works with the violet ray, which brings people into closer alignment with the soul.

Lithotherapy

- Known as a magical and mysterious stone
- Stimulates inner vision and spiritual intuition
- Creates a bridge between the crown and heart chakras, thereby purifying the aura and encouraging unconditional love
- Facilitates connections with other spiritual dimensions while remaining anchored
- Purifies and transmutes negativity
- Arouses profound emotional healing
- Helps one to accept the present moment
- Encourages acknowledging one's faults and tolerating those of others
- Confers direction, vigor, and spontaneity
- Diminishes stress and worries
- Helps to overcome compulsions and obsessions
- Encourages autonomous decision making for those too influenced by others
- Rejuvenates following exhaustion
- Regularizes blood pressure
- Supports the eyes
- Treats the heart, liver, and pancreas
- Alleviates cramps and pain
- Relieves insomnia and grants peaceful sleep to children
- Treats autism and bipolar disorders

Known as the "Stone of Transformation" or the "Stone of the Soul," charoite is a powerful transmuter of fears, which block progress and growth. It can be worn in contact with the heart chakra, placed at the third eye for short intervals, or placed directly on the skin wherever its energy is required.

CHRYSOCOLLA

Crystal System: monoclinic

Colors: blue turquoise, green

Chakras: third eye, throat, heart, solar plexus, hara

Hardness: 2.5

Origin: Chile, Democratic Republic of the Congo, Peru, Russia, United States (Arizona and Nevada)

Formation Process: sedimentary

Chemical Composition: hydrated copper silicate

Purification: cold water, incense, sunlight

Recharging: quartz cluster, sunlight

Generalities

Chrysocolla is a feminine energy and is known as the younger sister to her brother, turquoise. It symbolizes beauty, love and harmony. A force resides in its softness, acting to elevate the consciousness of those who work with it.

Lithotherapy

- Favors equanimity and self-observation
- Helps one to accept ever-changing situations and to strive toward goals
- Gives momentum when one is lethargic and calms an overactive nervous system when one is agitated
- Helps to maintain a cool head
- Helps one to discern what promotes evolution and growth of the consciousness and what retards and regresses one's potential
- Eases feelings of guilt and encourages forgiveness
- Harmonizes groups and environments

- Fights infections, in particular of the throat and tonsils
- Reduces inflammation of sinuses, tonsils, larynx, and lungs
- Detoxifies and reinforces the liver, kidneys, and colon
- Regularizes the nervous system and heart
- Balances sugar levels and treats the pancreas
- Balances the hormones and soothes premenstrual ailments and menstrual pains
- Lowers the body temperature in case of fever
- Reduces tension and promotes relaxation
- Fortifies the muscles and alleviates cramps
- Accelerates the healing of burns
- Normalizes the functioning of the thyroid
- Alleviates digestive problems caused by stress
- Treats ulcers

Placed on the solar plexus chakra, chrysocolla roots out negative emotions; on the heart chakra, it treats grief and sorrow and intensifies the capacity to love. Placed on the throat chakra, it improves communication while encouraging discernment. Placed on the third eye, it can clear negative thoughts and improve inner vision.

CHRYSOPRASE

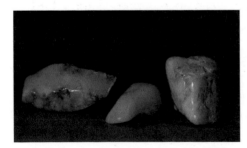

Crystal System: trigonal

Colors: yellow, clear green to deep green

Chakras: heart, solar plexus

Hardness: 6.5 to 7

Origin: Australia, India, Madagascar, Russia, South Africa, United States

Formation Process: sedimentary

Chemical Composition: silicon oxide

Purification: cold water, salt water, incense, abundant sunlight, earth

Recharging: quartz cluster, sunlight

Generalities

Chrysoprase is the stone of spring and of new life cycles. Known as a "stone of truth," it allows perception into hidden motives behind speech and actions.

Lithotherapy

- Favors a profound state of meditation
- Encourages the cultivation of a compassionate nature
- Stimulates appreciation of beauty and art
- Opens the mind to new ways of doing things in a variety of situations
- Activates foresight and flexibility
- Provides a sense of security and trust
- Diminishes anger, jealousy, envy, miserliness, and egotism
- Acts to stimulate and purify the heart chakra, helping one to heal from past relationships
- Balances masculine and feminine polarities
- Favors nonjudgment, stimulating acceptance of oneself and others
- Helps to eliminate negative attitudes by directing attention to positive events
- Contributes to freeing oneself from feelings and attitudes of superiority or inferiority
- Develops self-confidence and clarity of mind
- Fights against physical and mental exhaustion
- Stimulates the liver and detoxifies the body

- Reinforces reproductive organs
- Increases fertility
- Helps to treat gout and skin ailments
- Fortifies the thymus and lungs and treats heart problems

CITRINE

Crystal System: trigonal

Color: yellow

Chakra: solar plexus

Hardness: 7

Origin: Brazil, Madagascar, Russia

Formation Process: magmatic

Chemical Composition: silicon dioxide and iron

Purification: cold water, salt water, incense, sunlight, earth

Recharging: quartz cluster, sunlight

Generalities

Citrine is known to attract wealth, abundance, and prosperity. Authentic citrine is becoming more and more difficult to find and much of it is actually radiated amethyst. The key to distinguishing the real from the false is the color. Pure citrine is a light yellow crystal, whereas heated amethyst is far darker and more opaque. The properties of heated amethyst are similar to those of real citrine, though less effective.

Lithotherapy

· Purifies the aura by filling the dark spaces with light

· Stimulates the brain and reinforces the intellect

· Encourages new ideas and stimulates creativity in order to resolve problems more easily

· Favors the expression of individuality

· Grants confidence, courage, and dynamism

· Vibrates an energy of wealth and abundance in order to attract what is naturally our due

· Protects from snake venom and negative thoughts

· Supports sensitive and vulnerable people

· Stimulates the desire for change, for new experiences and self-realization

· Encourages a joy of living and elevates the spirits

· Soothes family or group discord

· Contributes to overcoming depression and oppressive influences

· Encourages extroversion and favors self-expression

· Enhances the capacity for rapid understanding

· Stimulates digestion and the proper functioning of the stomach, spleen, and pancreas

· Alleviates diabetes

· Relieves bladder infections

· Reinforces the nerves

· Generates inner heat within the body

· Relieves constipation and dissolves cellulite

A citrine invites the golden ray of the Spirit into the physical realm. It is recommended to place a citrine in a corner of a room, preferably in the left corner that is the most distant from the door, as this is known as the corner of wealth.

Coral Family

Crystal System: none available

Colors: white, black, orange, pink, red

Chakras: heart, root, third eye

Hardness: 3 to 4

Origin: Australia, Biscayne Bay, Canary Islands, Japan, Malaya, Mediterranean and Red Seas

Formation Process: unknown

Chemical Composition: calcium carbonate

Purification: requires no purification as it does not hold negative energy

Recharging: none required

Generalities

Coral is a living organic structure that exists in warm waters and acts as a home to numerous sea creatures. It is composed of a colony of polyps on a limestone base. Considered as a skeleton, it is frequently used in surgery for bone transplants, fractures, or bone cancers.

Lithotherapy

· Links one to water's purifying and revitalizing force

· Protects against negative influences

· Brushes aside negative thoughts

· Aids with visualization and meditation

· Possesses a strong calming effect

· Fortifies the bones

· Fights anemia following disease or due to a weakened immune system

- Favors blood circulation throughout the body but especially in the legs
- Helps fortify the blood when on a low-animal protein diet
- Relieves insomnia
- Relieves depression and increases energy
- Favors mental and physical health
- Acts as a sexual stimulant for men (orange type)

Black Coral

Coral, amethyst, mother of pearl

Lithotherapy

- Helps to calm fears and panic in crisis
- Stimulates imagination and poetic creativity
- Confers kindness and sensitivity
- Stimulates the mind
- Brings awareness to the subconscious levels of the mind

- Favors premonition in the dream state and helps to recall dreams
- Protects from negative energy and helps overcome depression
- Purifies the blood
- Regulates the circulatory system

Pink Coral

Lithotherapy

· Helps to overcomes emotional conflicts

· Contributes to overcoming panic and fear

Red Coral

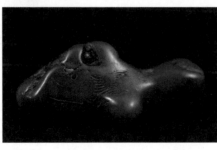

Lithotherapy

· Composed of cosmic energy

· Confers force and courage

· Combines the strengths of the three realms: mineral, vegetable, and animal

· Helps to increase personal magnetism

· Balances mood swings

· Prevents storms and guards against poisoning

· Promotes long life and a warm heart

· Alleviates nightmares

· Contributes to reinforcing the whole body

· Favors tooth growth for children

- Fortifies the muscular system
- Reduced to powder, it favors the lactation process in pregnant women
- Increases the capacity of bone marrow to produce red blood vessels
- Encourages the process of oxygen absorption in the lungs
- Relieves hemorrhoids and varicose veins
- Stimulates blood clotting in the case of wounds

Legend has it that when red coral pales, a disease may be forthcoming. Furthermore, when stains appear, it is said to be a sign of imminent death.

DANBURITE

Crystal System: rhombic

Colors: colorless, light blue, light pink, translucent gold

Chakras: heart, crown

Hardness: 7 to 7.5

Origin: Burma, Japan, Madagascar, Mexico, United States

Formation Process: magmatic

Chemical Composition: boron and calcium silicate

Purification: cold water, incense, early morning sunlight, earth

Recharging: quartz cluster, early morning sunlight

Generalities

Danburite is a stone which holds spiritual virtues. It lends assistance to one's inner path of growth and awareness.

Lithotherapy

- Acts on the heart energy
- Endowed with a very pure vibration
- Activates the intellect and higher consciousness, helping one to connect to the angelic realm
- Bridges heaven and heart, linking one to the divine consciousness
- Aligns the heart chakra with the higher chakras
- Liberates from karmic cycles and helps with the process of transformation
- Balances the brain hemispheres
- Alleviates blockages in the meridians
- Invites light into the aura and favors lucid dreams
- Opens the heart and incites self-love (pink danburite)
- Treats liver and gallbladder problems
- Eliminates bodily toxins
- Alleviates allergies and eases chronic conditions
- Favors weight gain if necessary
- Fortifies muscular and motor functions

When placed near the bed, danburite accompanies a dying person through his or her journey beyond death, allowing for a conscious spiritual transition. To stimulate lucid dreaming, it is recommended to place a danburite under one's pillow. To prevent different types of illness, place it wherever it is needed.

Desert Rose (Desert Stone)

Crystal System: monoclinic

Color: sand (pink brown)

Chakras: root, solar plexus

Hardness: 1.5 to 2

Origin: Morocco, Tunisia, United States deserts (Arizona, New Mexico)

Formation Process: sedimentary

Chemical Composition: hydrated calcium sulfate

Purification: incense, sunlight, avoid water as much as possible

Recharging: quartz cluster, sunlight

Generalities

Belonging to the selenite family, the desert rose possesses the qualities of that particular family in addition to its own specific characteristics.

Lithotherapy

- Encourages freedom from self-imposed psychological programming
- Facilitates the substitution of unhealthy indoctrination with more appropriate programming
- Reinforces the power of affirmations in order to achieve specific goals
- Encourages all forms of communication
- Permits one to see through lies and behind facades
- Acts as a tool for psychic communication
- Facilitates recall of dreams and past lives

DIAMOND

Crystal System: cubic

Colors: from yellow to brown, black, light blue, colorless, light pink, rarely green

Chakras: crown, third eye

Hardness: 10

Origin: Australia, Brazil, Russia, South Africa

Formation Process: metamorphic

Chemical Composition: carbon

Purification: cold water, salt water, incense, sunlight, earth

Recharging: quartz cluster, sunlight

Generalities

The name "diamond" comes from the Greek word "adamas" which means "invincible." It symbolizes force, courage, and immunity. Being a particularly powerful stone, the diamond can accentuate one's qualities as much as one's faults. Hence, this stone should be used with caution and with full awareness of its capacity.

When using a diamond in lithotherapy, it is recommended to place a black tourmaline at the root chakra for grounding purposes.

Lithotherapy

· Contributes to inner transformation and unification

· Acts as a powerful purifier

· Increases the power of other stones

· Encourages the fusion of personality and soul

· Amplifies thought forms

· Purifies the energy body

· Prevents the formation of kidney and gallbladder stones

· Fortifies the bladder

· Favors the healing of wounds

· Reinforces the immune activity of the thymus

· Alleviates the impact of bone diseases

· Acts as a treatment for gout

DIOPTASE

Crystal System: trigonal

Colors: dark blue, emerald green

Chakra: heart

Hardness: 5

Origin: Chile, Democratic Republic of the Congo, Iran, Namibia, North Africa, Peru, Russia, United States

Formation Process: sedimentary

Chemical Composition: hydrated copper silicate

Purification: cold water, salt water, incense, sunlight, earth (required before each treatment)

Recharging: quartz cluster, sunlight

Generalities

Legend has it that dioptase is related to Venus and thus symbolizes beauty. This stone, also called "copper emerald," was formerly considered a stone of wealth and abundance.

Lithotherapy

- Heals the heart chakra
- Favors the inflow of elevated energies into the heart chakra
- Draws in a new vibration of love at all levels
- Assists in reaching a higher state of consciousness
- Encourages one to live in the present while also activating memories of past lives
- Supports the awareness of our own inner wealth
- Facilitates service to others
- Helps to emphasize innate faculties and guides towards self-realization
- Invigorates imagination and creative ideas
- Has the power to change negative into positive in all aspects of life
- Guides one toward the needed direction, especially when the direction is unclear and one doesn't know where to go
- Clarifies and purifies thoughts
- Lessens the tendency to control others
- Contributes to healing the emotional wounds of the inner child
- Dissolves and heals the feelings of grief, betrayal, sadness, and abandonment
- Fights dependency and stress
- Heals trauma and nervous shock
- Teaches that difficulties in relationships are the reflection of an inner separation from the higher self
- Activates liver regeneration
- Eases pain, cramps, nausea, and chronic headaches
- Regularizes cellular disorders
- Activates T cells and the thymus
- Contributes to relieving arterial hypertension
- Treats cardiac problems

EMERALD

Crystal System: hexagonal

Color: from yellowish green to blue green

Chakra: heart

Hardness: 7.5 to 8

Origin: Australia, Austria, Brazil, Colombia, India, Madagascar, Nigeria, Pakistan, Russia, South Africa, Tanzania, United States, Zambia

Formation Process: magmatic, metamorphic

Chemical Composition: aluminum and beryllium silicate

Purification: cold water, incense, sunlight, earth (rarely needed for the emerald absorbs very little negative energy)

Recharging: sunlight

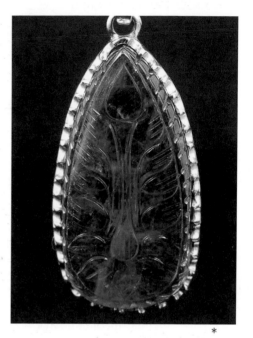

*

Generalities

The ancient civilizations of Europe and India considered the emerald to be the stone that conveyed divine inspiration. In antiquity, it was used to heal the eyes, whereas in the Middle Ages is was known to stop illnesses. When the emerald changed color, it was indicative of infidelity. Wearing an emerald continuously could trigger negative emotions in some individuals.

Lithotherapy

- Conveys inspiration and infinite patience
- Represents fulfilled love
- Grants domestic bliss and loyalty
- Confers frankness and the joy of living
- Acts as a guide towards one's goal
- Brings clarity and alertness, and encourages broad vision
- Strengthens unity, unconditional love, and partnership
- Generates mutual understanding in a group and stimulates cooperation
- Favors friendship
- Ensures physical, emotional, and mental balance
- Eliminates negativity and inspires positive actions
- Confers strength of character to overcome obstacles
- Eases symptoms of claustrophobia
- Confers the kind of wisdom that evokes discernment
- Activates rejuvenation and recovery
- Contributes to prompt recovery following an infectious disease
- Treats the sinuses, lungs, and heart
- Supports the spine and muscular system
- Improves eyesight
- Detoxifies the liver
- Relieves rheumatism and diabetes
- Is an antidote for poisons
- Alleviates epileptic attacks

EPIDOTE

Crystal System: monoclinic

Color: green

Chakras: heart, solar plexus

Hardness: 6 to 7

Origin: Austria, Mexico, Mozambique, Norway, United States (California)

Formation Process: magmatic, metamorphic

Chemical Composition: very complex basic calcaro-ferrous aluminosilicate

Purification: cold water, salt water, incense, sunlight, earth

Recharging: quartz cluster, sunlight

Generalities

Epidote amplifies the intrinsic characteristics of an individual. It fosters the development of positive attributes, but also amplifies the negative aspects, forcing one to make profound changes.

Lithotherapy

- Increases personal power
- Conveys the gift of initiative
- Favors positive interaction with others
- Diminishes tendencies to criticize self and others
- Facilitates the creation of realistic goals, all the while guiding toward success
- Encourages acceptance of one's own weakness while supporting self-esteem

- Contributes to overcoming self-destructive emotions that cause depression
- Facilitates recovery after illness, burnout, or stress
- Stimulates the desire for healthy, realistic, and positive changes that will bring success
- Regenerates and rejuvenates at all levels
- Works in favor of good health and overall well-being
- Develops and reinforces the immune system
- Assists in the proper functioning of the digestive system, especially the gallbladder, liver, and small intestine
- Relieves heartburn
- Treats the nervous system
- Reinforces the thyroid gland
- Relieves brain disorders
- Softens the skin (especially when taken as an elixir)

FLUORITE FAMILY

Crystal System: cubic

Colors: all the colors of the spectrum

Chakras: according to color

Hardness: 4

Origin: England, France, Germany

Formation Process: magmatic

Chemical Composition: calcium fluoride

Purification: cold water, incense, sunlight, earth

Recharging: quartz cluster, sunlight

Generalities

Because it supports the learning process, fluorite is the perfect stone for students. Fluorite is also an excellent stone to counteract the effects of electromagnetic fog produced by computers, microwaves, and televisions.

Lithotherapy

- Is highly protective, especially on a psychic level
- Known as an etheric healer, it purifies and stabilizes the aura
- Fosters the development of spiritual awareness by stimulating the creation and expression of the highest abstract concepts
- Heightens the spirit of invention and the process of creation on the basis of freedom of decision
- Brings awareness to repressed feelings and allows for their gradual expression
- Calms the emotions, promotes self-confidence, and dispels confusion
- Helps to eliminate rooted attitudes, obsessions, and narrow-mindedness
- Acts against character flaws
- Quickens the mental processing and organizing of information
- Stimulates learning
- Reinforces concentration and rational thought
- Favors swift comprehension and quick thinking
- Expels negative energy and stress
- Contributes to energy transmissions
- Purifies, dispels, and reorganizes energies in the body
- Reinforces the immune system
- Stimulates the regeneration of skin and mucous membranes, especially in the lungs and respiratory tract
- Supports in cases of tumors, ulcers, and purulent wounds

- Fortifies bones, teeth, and cells

- Repairs damage to the DNA

- Treats deformities of the body

- Confers mobility to the body, diminishes stiffness and joint problems (such as arthritis)

- Enhances the activity of the nervous system, particularly that of the brain

- Alleviates allergies that have a psychological cause

- Aids digestion

- Guards against anorexia

- Activates blood circulation

- Acts on muscle tone and toxin elimination, hence especially recommended for athletes

- Benefits the spleen

Fluorite should be worn directly on the skin. It has a tendency to absorb a lot, and it is therefore preferable to cleanse and charge it after each use. Fluorite has additional properties related to its particular color and may be placed on a chakra accordingly.

BLUE FLUORITE

*

Lithotherapy

- Facilitates spiritual awakening

- Balances the throat chakra

- Enhances creative and logical thought as well as clear communication

- Calms and revitalizes the biomagnetic field

- Is beneficial for eye, nose, ear, and throat problems

- Amplifies curative potentials by activating or intensifying dormant activities in the brain

- Reduces inflammation (such as rheumatoid arthritis)

CLEAR FLUORITE

Lithotherapy

- Stimulates the crown chakra

- Charges the aura with energy

- Balances the mind

- Aligns the chakras, allowing universal energy to penetrate the body

*

- Reinforces the effects of other crystals during the healing process

- Improves impaired vision

GREEN FLUORITE

Lithotherapy

- Aligns the heart chakra

- Anchors excessive energy

- Dissipates emotional traumas

- Eliminates infections

- Absorbs negative energies from the environment

- Gives access to information from the subconscious and opens the door to intuition

- Purifies the aura, the chakras, and the mind

- Relieves gastric problems and intestinal cramps

Violet or Purple Fluorite

Lithotherapy

· Stimulates the third eye

· Confers common sense and discrimination during psychic communication

· Supports meditation

· Contributes to the treatment of bones and bone marrow ailments

Yellow Fluorite

Lithotherapy

· Enhances creativity and stabilizes group energy

· Supports cooperation

· Favors intellectual activities

· Eliminates toxins and soothes the liver

· Treats cholesterol imbalances

Garnet Family

Crystal System: cubic

Colors: black, brown, green, orange, pink, red, yellow, and sometimes purplish

Chakras: according to color

Hardness: 6.5 to 7.5

Origin: Afghanistan, Austria, Brazil, Czechoslovakia, India, Sri Lanka

Formation Process: metamorphic

Chemical Composition: aluminum and iron silicate

Purification: cold water, salt water, incense, sunlight, earth (recommended before or after each use)

Recharging: quartz cluster, sunlight

Generalities

In the Middle Ages, warriors set their shields and sword hilts in garnet to protect themselves from wounds. Garnet was also worn as an amulet in order to attract happiness, wealth, and blessings.

Lithotherapy

- · Illumines the soul
- · Sheds light and gives hope when life seems hopeless
- · Instills energy and regenerates the body
- · Purifies, recharges, and revitalizes the chakras
- · Balances energies, generating either serenity or passion, accordingly
- · Inspires love and devotion
- · Balances sexual desire and appeases emotional turmoil
- · Stimulates the rise of appropriate kundalini energy and sustains virility

- Strengthens the survival instinct and transforms crisis into challenge
- Facilitates mutual assistance
- Encourages dynamism, promotes action, and perseverance
- Revives awareness and memory of past lives (both related to the processes of the pituitary gland)
- Brings success in business (square-cut garnet)
- Helps to overcome resistance or persistent self-sabotage, and contributes to dissolving obsolete behaviors
- Removes inhibitions and taboos
- Opens the heart
- Boosts self-confidence

Garnet can be worn as a necklace or pendant. It is important that the stone be in contact with the skin. When placed at the third eye, garnet may revive past-life memories.

ALMANDINE GARNET (RED TO BROWN, SOMETIMES PURPLISH)

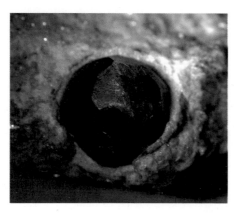

Lithotherapy

- Confers strength and power (regenerative stone)
- May result in harmful outcomes if used on quick-tempered or highly stressed individuals
- Encourages taking time for oneself
- Teaches charity and compassion
- Generates the birth of profound love

- Opens the channel between the root and crown chakras
- Facilitates the absorption of iron in the intestines
- Treats the liver and pancreas

ANDRADITE GARNET (YELLOWISH GREEN)

Lithotherapy

· Promotes dynamism and flexibility

· Stimulates creativity

· Attracts love affairs

*

· Encourages the development of masculine qualities such as courage, vigor, and force

· Purifies the aura

· Contributes to blood production

· Effective in restoring the proper functioning of the liver, gallbladder, and intestines

· Contributes to calcium, magnesium and iron absorption

· Activates the healing process of fractures and skin disorders

GROSSULAR GARNET (DARK ORANGE TO BROWN ORANGE)

Lithotherapy

· Strengthens and fortifies the bone structure

· Reinforces one's strength in times of dejection

· Helps to meet challenges and brings support during trials and tribulations

· Is conducive to relaxation

· Inspires cooperation

· Increases fertility

· Facilitates vitamin A assimilation

- Strengthens renal function
- Contributes to the regeneration of the skin and mucous membranes
- Drains the body of encumbrances such as fat deposits

HESSONITE GARNET (RED ORANGE TO RED BROWN)

Lithotherapy

- Assists one to develop self-respect
- Fosters spiritual growth
- Calms unsatisfied sexual desires
- Dissolves guilt and feelings of inferiority
- Encourages service to others
- Eliminates negative influences that undermine health

- Contributes to regulating hormone production
- Treats sterility and impotence
- Benefits the olfactory system

MELANITE GARNET (DARK BROWN TO BLACK)

*

Lithotherapy

- Protects and stabilizes
- Fosters honesty and candor
- Increases strength, particularly the strengthening of the spine and bones

- Facilitates the body's adaptation to medical treatment
- Collaborates with cancer treatments
- Eases apoplexy crises
- Treats rheumatism and arthritis
- Eliminates blockages in the heart and throat chakras
- Treats heart disease
- When associated with carnelian, it eases circulatory problems in the legs and uterus

PYROPE GARNET (BLOOD RED TO RED BROWN)

Lithotherapy

- Inspires courage
- Intensifies charisma
- Favors a high quality of life
- Stimulates the root chakra, raising earth energies to higher centers

*

- Stimulates creativity
- Aligns the crown and root chakras with the subtle bodies
- Effective in fighting nervous breakdown and fatigue
- Confers vitality
- Improves blood circulation and blood quality
- Calms heartburn
- Soothes sore throats
- Treats anemia
- Regulates heart troubles, blood pressure, and blood circulation
- Vitalizes the sexual organs

Red Garnet

Lithotherapy

· Represents love and resonates with the heart energy

· Revives blocked feelings

· Intensifies sexuality

· Helps in anger management, most specifically when anger is aimed at oneself

Rhodolite Garnet (rose red, magenta to purplish)

*

Lithotherapy

· Invites liveliness, warmth, and trust

· Stimulates the intuition and inspiration

· Generates a healthy sexuality

· Reinforces the metabolism

· Treats the heart, lungs, and hips

· Excels in detoxification and treats blood poisoning

Spessartite Garnet (orange, red, brown)

Lithotherapy

· Encourages service to others

· Inculcates the will to help others

· Acts as an antidepressant

· Alleviates nightmares

*

· Treats sexual problems, especially for those who have experienced abuse and trauma (a stone to be used in moderation)

· Eliminates feelings of guilt

· Fortifies the heart

· Treats intolerance to lactose and malfunctions in calcium absorption

· Excels in the treatment of anorexia, as it revives the appetite

Tsavorite Garnet (various shades of dark green)

Lithotherapy

· Presents a very powerful yet short-lasting effect

· Relieves acute pain

Uvarovite Garnet (emerald green with shades of green yellow)

Lithotherapy

· Eliminates feelings of inadequacy

· Promotes individuality and enthusiasm

· Encourages one to live in the present

· Releases emotional blockages, helping one to regain sensitivity and trust

· Fortifies spiritual relationships

· Stimulates the heart chakra

· Contributes to detoxification

· Acts as an anti-inflammatory

· Soothes fevers

· Treats acidosis (high acidity of the blood plasma)

· Supports treatments of leukemia

· Stimulates low sexual libido

· Balances high blood pressure

· Supports the liver through its purifying effect on the blood

Gem Silica

Crystal System: monoclinic

Colors: blue, turquoise, translucent green

Chakras: heart, throat, third eye

Hardness: 6 to 7

Origin: Peru, United States

Formation Process: sedimentary

Chemical Composition: hydrated copper silicate

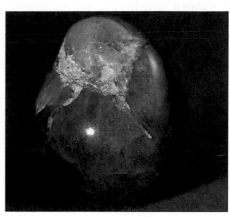

Purification: cold water, incense, sunlight, earth

Recharging: rarely required—incense and quartz cluster at one's discretion

Generalities

Gem Silica is, in fact, a gem-quality chrysocolla. It is a combination of chrysocolla and quartz.

Lithotherapy

- Is one of the most refined stones to treat the throat chakra
- Encourages self-expression and allows for a clear and eloquent conveyance of truth
- Encourages the locution of one's inner truth
- Acts gently, though it possesses great power
- Facilitates a concrete manifestation of feminine power by calling upon the energy of the Goddess
- Possesses the ability to evoke past-life memories
- Awakens imaginative and creative abilities
- Allows one to let go of what oppresses the psyche

- Increases emotional discernment, directing one's focus to what is essential in life and in relationships
- Alleviates depression and feelings of self-deprecation
- Heightens inner vision and clairvoyance
- Enhances telepathic communication
- Balances and soothes the emotional body
- Seals holes in the astral and etheric bodies, especially in the area of the heart
- Amplifies the effectiveness of prayers, chants, and mantras by augmenting the power and purity of words and sound vibrations
- Stimulates and clears the third eye
- Contributes to the proper functioning of the respiratory system
- Helps in case of bronchitis and asthma
- Treats diseases of the vocal cords

Halite Family

Crystal System: cubic

Colors: white, blue, clear, gray

Chakras: according to color

Hardness: 2 to 2.5

Origin: Algeria, Austria, Canada, China, Ethiopia, France, Great Britain, India, Peru, Poland, Siberia, Sicily, Southwest Africa, Spain, Switzerland, United States

Formation Process: sedimentary

Chemical Composition: sodium chloride

Purification: Not required since halite does not absorb negative energies; contact with water must be avoided to prevent disintegration

Recharging: sunlight

Generalities

Halite is a salt stone that acts as a powerful purifier of discordant and impure vibrations, replacing them with more favorable energies. Considering its low cost, it may be used as bath salt, diffusing its beneficial properties into the water.

BLUE HALITE

Blue and clear halite

Lithotherapy

Blue halite contains deep blue, violet, and white hues and therefore possesses the properties of each of these colors.

· Purifies the energy field

· Activates psychic abilities

· Elevates the consciousness to the highest of spiritual realms

· Activates the third-eye and crown chakras

· Aligns energies wherever it is placed

· Releases blockages in all superior chakras, particularly the throat

· Quickly frees the mind from worries and thoughts

· Opens the door to communication with the world of Spirit and with one's inner guides

· Encourages the verbal expression of spiritual truths

· Purifies other stones and crystals

· Provides support during fasts or other types of bodily purifications

· Resonates particularly well with the lymphatic and blood systems

· Contributes to the elimination of toxins and metals from the body

Clear Halite

Lithotherapy

- Purifies and illuminates the energy body
- Dissolves the energetic density that hinders the light of the soul from being integrated into the gross and subtle bodies

Pink Halite

Lithotherapy

- Purifies the heart
- Assists in overcoming past emotional traumas
- Opens up the heart and facilitates union with the source of universal Love
- Facilitates self-love
- Supports and encourages a healthy lifestyle
- Calms and soothes the solar plexus
- Dissolves blockages between the solar plexus and the heart, thereby elevating energies
- Dissolves confusion, disappointment, and doubt
- Allows one to discern the truth in a variety of situations
- Triggers an understanding of emotional patterns hidden behind life's experiences

Yellow Halite

Lithotherapy

· Purifies the aura

· Increases the vitality of the physical body

· Favors learning and improves memory

· Encourages discipline and steadfastness

Hawk Eye

Crystal System: trigonal

Colors: shimmering nuances of blue-gray and green gray blue

Chakras: throat, third eye

Hardness: 7

Origin: Australia, Brazil, Burma, India, South Africa, United States

Formation Process: magmatic

Chemical Composition: silicon oxide

Purification: cold water, salt water, incense, moonlight, sunlight, earth

Recharging: quartz cluster, moonlight, sunlight

Generalities

The asbestos fibers contained within the hawk eye create a silky reflection that resembles an eye. During the Middle Ages, this stone was thought to protect its bearer and allow him or her to perceive impending dangers. Hence it was worn as an amulet to protect against evil spells and the "evil eye."

Lithotherapy

- Awakens the appreciation for knowledge and research
- Opens the mind to new ideas and modes of thinking
- Confers a keen and alert mind
- Conveys a broad vision for projects
- Increases observation skills
- Encourages active listening and understanding
- Supports the capacity to see with precision and sustained attention
- Provides a clear view of complicated situations
- Assists with decision making
- Eliminates doubts
- Reinforces self-confidence by activating the will
- Generates enthusiasm
- Activates the throat chakra and facilitates oral expression
- Grants luck and abundance
- Eliminates nightmares
- Protects from harmful influences
- Provides an understanding of the "greater plan" in reference to one's personal life
- Reveals repressed emotions and pains from present and past lives
- Exposes the source of emotional blockages
- Promotes healthy detachment from one's emotions
- Helps to disengage oneself from negativity that causes mood swings
- Tempers pessimism and eliminates the desire to blame others for one's problems
- Contributes to healing the earth and aids one to remain anchored to the physical plane
- Develops intuition and facilitates clairvoyance

- Purifies and energizes the root chakra
- Reveals the psychosomatic causes of certain physical maladies
- Treats inflammatory eye problems, visual fatigue, conjunctivitis, and cataracts
- Relieves migraines
- Balances the thyroid gland
- Regulates breathing and purifies the bronchial tubes
- Eases pain
- Alleviates ailments related to the voice
- Calms nervousness and trembling
- Treats cases of hyperstimulation of hormonal glands
- Calms an overactive libido

HEMATITE

Crystal System: trigonal

Color: metallic gray

Chakra: root

Hardness: 5 to 6

Origin: Brazil, United States

Formation Process: magmatic, metamorphic

Chemical Composition: iron oxide

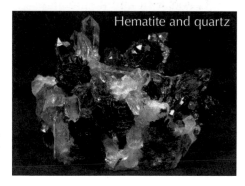
Hematite and quartz

Purification: cold water, sunlight, earth

Recharging: quartz cluster, sunlight

Generalities

Hematite was used in ancient Egypt to facilitate the development of red blood cells and to stop hemorrhaging. For this reason, it inherited the name "blood stone" during the Middle Ages.

Lithotherapy

· Grounds and reinforces the connection with the earth

· Confers feelings of safety and confidence

· Provides strength, courage, stamina, and vitality

· Eliminates and transmutes negative energies in the root chakra

· Protects from the negativity of others

· Encourages optimism and increases personal magnetism

· Facilitates healthy blood regeneration

· Stops hemorrhaging

· Increases blood quality and reduces blood pressure

· Stimulates iron absorption in the small intestine, as well as red blood cell formation

· Treats anemia

· Improves oxygen absorption and stabilizes the health

· Alleviates insomnia, restlessness, stress, and anxiety

· Decreases body temperature during a fever

· Relieves muscular pain due to skeletal problems

· Treats problems related to the skeletal system, such as arthritis, leg cramps, and fractures

· Assists in purifying the blood in the kidneys

· Regenerates tissues

· Reinforces the physical and etheric bodies

Hematite is to be avoided in the case of active inflammation, as it may worsen this condition. It facilitates alignment of the spinal column when one piece is placed at the top of the spine and one at the bottom. It is advisable to place or maintain hematite directly on the skin, depending on the need. It is, however, not advisable to use it for prolonged periods of time.

HERKIMER DIAMOND

Crystal System: trigonal

Color: transparent

Chakras: third eye, crown

Hardness: 7.5

Origin: Mexico, Spain, Tanzania, United States

Formation Process: magmatic

Chemical Composition: silicon oxide

Purification: salt water, rinse under running water

Recharging: quartz cluster, abundance of morning sunlight

Generalities

The herkimer is often called "herkimer diamond" due to its unusual clarity and brilliance. It is a small and stubby biterminated quartz emanating a surprisingly powerful vibration.

Lithotherapy

· Holds a powerful amplifying potential

· Stimulates telepathy, clairvoyance, out-of-body experiences and other psychic abilities

· Enhances meditation and inner vision

· Promotes dream recall, conscious and premonitory dreaming

- Activates one's connection to the higher self, angels, and higher spiritual realms
- Confers access to information from past lives, hence revealing the source of blockages that may impede spiritual growth
- Activates the light body
- Facilitates spiritual transformation, while focusing on the soul's purpose
- Confers hope and courage
- Augments the capacity of the body to integrate light and higher frequencies
- Promotes creativity
- Grants felicity and beatitude
- Purifies the chakras as well as the physical, etheric and other subtle bodies
- Protects against negative energies in one's living environment
- A powerful regenerator, it accelerates the healing process
- Removes energetic blockages and eliminates debris in the energetic field
- Protects against radiation and electromagnetic pollution
- Balances physical and mental energies
- When placed at the crown chakra, it creates a fusion with the divine and contributes to understanding one's life mission
- Placed near deceased individuals, it guides them to reconnect with their soul family
- Harmonizes therapist and client
- Augments physical energy and endurance
- Appeases tensions and worries
- Purifies and harmonizes the body
- Eliminates stress and muscular tension
- Fortifies the muscles

- Helps to correct DNA and metabolic imbalances as well as cellular malformations
- Helps in cases of eye troubles such as cataracts
- Supports in cases of hemophilia

Herkimer is a good stone to wear either as a pendent or as earrings.

HOWLITE

Crystal System: monoclinic

Colors: white, blue, green

Chakra: third eye

Hardness: 3.5

Origin: Canada, Germany, United States

Formation Process: sedimentary

Chemical Composition: calcium and boron silicate

Purification: water, incense

Recharging: quartz cluster, limited sunlight

Generalities

Howlite is often confused with turquoise. It is to be noted, however, that blue howlite is artificially colored.

Lithotherapy

- Soothes and calms
- Acts as an antidote against insomnia caused by an overagitated mind
- Allows the mind to open up to spiritual dimensions in order to develop intuition

- Inspires the creation of ambitions and activates their realization
- Facilitates out-of-body experiences into past or in-between lives
- Encourages patience and helps to eliminate rage and uncontrollable anger
- Contributes to diminishing selfish tendencies and negative criticism
- Reinforces positive personality traits
- Supports meditation
- Facilitates dream recollection
- Revives the memory and increases the desire for knowledge
- Calms turbulent emotions coming from past lives
- Balances calcium levels in the body
- Contributes to the healthy preservation of bones, teeth, and soft tissues

IOLITE

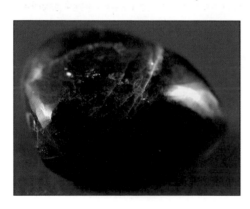

Crystal System: rhombic

Colors: blue, yellow, gray, violet

Chakra: third eye

Hardness: 7 to 7.5

Origin: Brazil, Burma, India, Madagascar, Sri Lanka, United States

Formation Process: magmatic

Chemical Composition: magnesium and aluminosilicate

Purification: quartz cluster, cold water, salt water, incense, abundance of sunlight

Recharging: quartz cluster, abundance of sunlight

Generalities

Iolite has a particular affinity with the era of the Templar knights, the Cathars, and the legend of King Arthur. It is a stone of high spirituality and vision.

Lithotherapy

· Activates the third eye

· Enhances visualization and intuition

· Facilitates access to inner wisdom

· Contributes to the integration of common thinking with intuitive knowing

· Possesses the capacity to unlock the gateways of memory in order to integrate lessons and information acquired in past lives

· Offers support during out-of-body travels

· Encourages the creative expression of spiritual ideas and ideals

· Dissolves the fear of the unknown and repressed aspects of psyche

· Produces an electrical jolt that heightens the vibrational level of the auric field

· Aligns the subtle bodies

· Brings an understanding and a release of the causes of addictive behaviors

· Encourages free expression of the higher self, regardless of what others may say or think

· Clarifies thoughts

· Eases discord in relationships

· Promotes responsibility

· Alleviates codependency in intimate relationships

· Strengthens the body structure

· Eliminates fat deposits from the body

· Diminishes the side effects of alcohol

- Detoxifies and regenerates the liver
- Fights malaria and fever
- Supports the pituitary gland, the sinuses, and the respiratory system
- Treats eye problems
- Alleviates migraines
- Eliminates unhealthy bacteria

JADE FAMILY

Crystal System: monoclinic

Colors: white, beige brown, red brown, green, purple blue, black

Chakra: heart

Hardness: 6.5 to 7

Origin: Burma, China, Guatemala, Japan, Mexico, United States

Formation Process: metamorphic

Chemical Composition: aluminum and sodium silicate

Purification: cold water, salt water, incense, sunlight, earth

Recharging: quartz cluster, sunlight

Generalities

In ancient times, jade was considered a sacred stone that brought good luck, prosperity, and long life.

Lithotherapy

- Preserves loving sentiments
- Facilitates dream interpretation
- Helps to resolve problems
- Instills compassion
- Contributes to spiritual realization
- Allows one to see oneself as a spiritual being
- Generates spontaneity in the organization of one's life
- Invigorates passive individuals
- Stimulates ideas and the need for action
- Soothes irritation
- Awakens hidden knowledge
- Purifies all the bodies and eliminates bodily toxins
- Treats the adrenal glands
- Balances the metabolism
- Accelerates recuperation from injuries
- Favors fertility and supports labor and delivery
- Stabilizes bodily fluids
- Is beneficial for heart problems
- Balances the nervous system

Jade can be worn as jewelry, or placed directly on the body. It collaborates with the dream process when placed on the forehead. According to Chinese tradition, jade transmits its virtues to whomever holds it in his or her hand.

Jade – Jadeite

Chemical Composition: aluminum and sodium silicate

Purification: salt water

Recharging: quartz cluster, sunlight

Lithotherapy

- · Inspires virtue
- · Confers tolerance
- · Represents the earthly manifestation of the cosmic male principle
- · Prolongs life
- · Regulates the activity of the kidneys and urinary system
- · Treats back pain

Lavender Jade

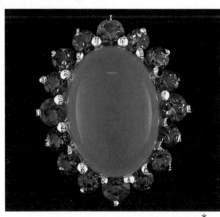

Purification: salt water

Recharging: quartz cluster, sunlight

Lithotherapy

- · Contributes to delineating one's limits
- · Alleviates emotional pain or trauma
- · Confers inner peace

*

MAGNETITE JADE

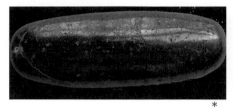

Chemical Composition: basic magnesium and calcium silicate, iron, and magnetite

Purification: cold water, incense, moonlight, sunlight, earth (requires more frequent purification than other kinds of jade)

Recharging: quartz cluster, sunlight, moonlight

Lithotherapy

- · Confers a prosperous life
- · Attracts success
- · Brings good fortune and is favorable in games of chance
- · Benefits the kidneys and bladder

NEPHRITE JADE

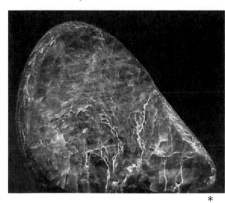

Chemical Composition: basic magnesium and calcium silicate, iron and magnetite

Purification: salt water, cold water

Recharging: quartz cluster, sunlight

Lithotherapy

- · Regulates the kidneys, the urinary system, and the adrenal glands
- · Contributes to eliminating kidney stones
- · Reduces incontinence and soothes cystitis

JASPER FAMILY

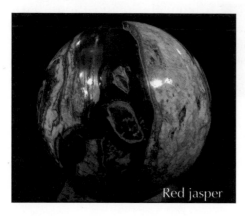
Red jasper

Crystal System: trigonal

Colors: black, brown, green, red, yellow

Chakras: according to color

Hardness: 6.5 to 7

Origin: Brazil, France, Germany, India

Formation Process: sedimentary

Chemical Composition: silicon oxide

Purification: cold water, salt water, incense, sunlight, earth

Recharging: quartz cluster, sunlight

Generalities

In ancient Egypt, jasper was used to make amulets on which scarab beetles were sculpted. In the Middle Ages, this stone was recognized as the stone of the warrior.

Lithotherapy

- · Is known as the "Supreme Protector"
- · Anchors energies within the body
- · Purifies and aligns the chakras
- · Absorbs negative energies
- · Assists in shamanic journeys
- · Facilitates the recall of dreams when placed under the pillow
- · Absorbs electromagnetic and environmental pollution
- · Confers courage and determination, encouraging a "warrior spirit"

- Favors self-honesty and candor
- Kindles mutual assistance
- Supports one in times of conflict
- Facilitates rapid reflection
- Contributes to the development of organizational abilities
- Stimulates imagination
- Transforms ideas into actions
- Supports during periods of stress or during long-lasting illness
- Benefits the digestive system, especially the gallbladder and liver
- Fortifies the circulatory system
- Supports the bladder and sexual organs
- Re-energizes the body
- Balances the mineral content of the body

Jasper is a stone that imparts an earthy, physical vibration and is a powerful therapeutic companion. It must be placed directly on the skin for effective results. Its energy is less intense and slower to act and may therefore be worn for long periods of time.

BLACK JASPER (1ˢᵗ CHAKRA)

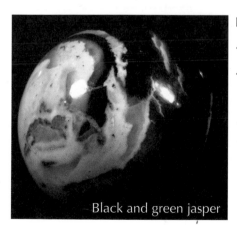
Black and green jasper

Lithotherapy

- Grounds one to reality
- Protects from negative energies

Blood or Heliotrope Jasper (1st and 4th chakras)
(See Bloodstone)

Brown Jasper

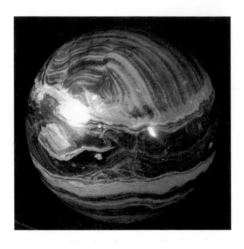

Lithotherapy

· Embodies the energy of Mother Earth

· Brings comfort and reduces fear

· Instills a sense of right proportion

· Inspires harmony

· Favors the unveiling of hidden feelings

· Stimulates the immune system

· Purifies the kidneys

Green Jasper (4th chakra)

Lithotherapy

· Balances the heart chakra

· Detoxifies the body

· Reinforces the immune system

· Provides an anti-inflammatory effect the entire body

· Protects against pollution

· Treats the lungs

RED JASPER (1st and 2nd CHAKRAS)

Lithotherapy

- Balances and anchors the root chakra
- Inspires physical vitality
- Conveys courage and will
- Strengthens the legs
- Activates circulation and increases energy
- Imparts good fortune to travelers

YELLOW JASPER (3rd CHAKRA)

*

Lithotherapy

- Helps one to persevere
- Stimulates the solar plexus chakra
- Eliminates toxins
- Treats the stomach and overall digestion
- Revives the endocrine system
- Calms the nerves
- Reinforces the immune system

Jet

Crystal System: amorphous

Color: black

Chakra: root

Hardness: 2.5 to 4

Origin: France, Great Britain, Spain, United States

Formation Process: sedimentary

Chemical Composition: silicon oxide

Purification: quartz cluster, cold water, incense, moonlight

Recharging: quartz cluster, moonlight

Generalities

Jet is known to be a powerful protector. Due to its texture and its light weight, jet is sometimes referred to as "black amber." It is, in fact, a carbon fossil that is formed from oceanic pressure on wood.

Lithotherapy

- Grounds and strengthens one's connection to the earth
- Sustains one during periods of mourning and solitude
- Protects against negative forces and curses
- Stimulates the awakening of the kundalini
- Absorbs inflammation caused by arthritis and rheumatism
- Prevents inflammation in the respiratory system
- Relieves toothaches and migraines
- Eases symptoms of epilepsy
- Soothes stomach pains and menstrual cramps
- Diminishes foot swelling if applied where the swelling predominates
- Confers elasticity to the body

KUNZITE

Crystal System: monoclinic

Colors: clear, green gray, pink violet, yellow

Chakras: heart, throat, third eye

Hardness: 6 to 7

Origin: Afghanistan, Brazil, Madagascar, Myanmar, Pakistan, United States (California)

Formation Process: magmatic

Chemical Composition: aluminium and lithium silicate

Purification: cold water, salt water, incense, earth (requires little purification)

Recharging: quartz cluster, no sunlight

Generalities

Kunzite is one of the best stones to offer as a gift as it opens the heart to divine love, self-love, love for others, of humanity, animals, plants, and minerals.

Lithotherapy

- Urges forgiveness
- Brings suppressed emotions to the surface, allowing us to face them
- Balances and calms emotions
- Allows one to be focused and calm when surrounded by many distractions
- Encourages wisdom and just actions
- Favors loving thoughts and communication while allowing suppressed feelings to be expressed in a constructive way

- Frees one from emotional dependency

- Facilitates maturity

- Encourages receptivity and connection to others

- Provides a protective shield against undesired energies

- Stimulates the heart chakra

- Encourages healthy love and self-respect

- Creates openness toward unconditional love

- Purifies the subtle bodies and facilitates profound meditation

- Reinforces the physical heart muscles and supports the lungs

- Encourages healthy blood circulation

- Balances calcium and magnesium levels in the body

Kunzite contains lithium and is therefore effective in calming anxiety and panic attacks. It can further help to balance depression and bipolar tendencies.

KYANITE (CYANITE OR DISTHENE)

Crystal System: triclinic

Colors: blue and white, gray, yellow, black, pink, green

Chakras: throat, third eye

Hardness: 4 to 5 in length; 7 in width

Origin: Brazil

Formation Process: metamorphic

Chemical Composition: aluminum silicate

Purification: cold water, incense, moonlight

Recharging: quartz cluster, moonlight

Generalities

Kyanite builds bridges of light between all aspects of experience. It particularly encourages connecting the head with the heart.

Lithotherapy

· Strengthens the throat chakra

· Instantaneously aligns the chakras and the subtle bodies, purifying meridians and other etheric channels

· Favors creative expression and communication

· Powerfully transmits and amplifies high-frequency energies, stimulating intuition and clairvoyance

· Removes the veils of ignorance to reveal spiritual and psychological truths

· Encourages awareness of the illusion behind blind fate or implacable karma

· Helps one to face the past with a balanced view

· Eases the transition during the dying process

· Calms anxious thoughts and feelings

· Favors a peaceful and pleasant mood

· Encourages the assertion of truth and surmounting of fears and obstacles

· Favors rational and logical thought and reinforces memory

· Benefits psychological problems and depressive tendencies

· Wards off confusion

· Alleviates inhibitions, inviting one to act spontaneously and with certainty when necessary

· Dissipates blockages from destructive emotions such as anger and impatience

· Encourages healthy curiosity

- Helps the mind to be of service to the heart
- Balances yin and yang energies
- Treats the brain, particularly reinforcing the proper functioning of the cerebellum and of the motor nerves, thereby improving mobility and agility
- Supports the throat, thyroid, and parathyroid glands
- Eases muscle pains
- Reinforces the urogenital system and adrenal glands
- Diminishes fever and high blood pressure
- Acts as a natural analgesic and treats infections

Kyanite has a penetrating energy that acts rapidly. It improves the therapist's intuition during treatment. It is advisable not to leave it in contact with sunlight, as it will lose its color and energy.

LABRADORITE

Crystal System: triclinic

Colors: gray, white, yellow, with slight blue, gold, and red reflections

Chakras: all

Hardness: 6 to 6.5

Origin: Australia, Canada, Madagascar, Mexico, Russia, United States

Formation Process: magmatic

Chemical Composition: calcium aluminosilicate

Purification: cold water, salt water, incense, early morning sunlight, earth

Recharging: quartz cluster, abundant early morning sunlight

Generalities

Labradorite is indispensable for those who work in public service and healing, such as medical professionals, social workers, therapists, teachers, and psychologists. It is known to provide a protective barrier, allowing one to serve wisely without losing too much energy or taking on the problems of those who are in need.

Lithotherapy

· A highly mystical stone

· Elevates the consciousness

· Acts as a bridge to universal energies

· Prevents energy leaks

· A powerful protector, forms a barrier against undesirable energies

· Dissolves illusions

· Clearly deploys all our objectives and intentions

· Stimulates intuition and psychic gifts

· Allows forgotten memories to resurface

· Provides a deepening of sentiments

· Stimulates imagination

· Encourages contemplation and interiorization

· Helps one to manifest childlike enthusiasm and favors an abundance of ideas

· Nourishes those who feel alone

· Provides support during periods of change

· Transmits strength and perseverance

· Balances body temperature, thereby reducing chills

· Treats rheumatism and gout

- Reduces tension and soothes
- Benefits eye and brain problems
- Balances hormones and relieves menstrual tension
- Powerfully regenerates when exhausted

Labradorite counters electromagnetic effects on the body that can come from devices such as televisions, microwave ovens, and computers.

Lapis Lazuli

Crystal System: cubic

Color: blue stippled with white

Chakras: throat, third eye

Hardness: 5 to 6

Origin: Afghanistan, Chile, Russia

Formation Process: metamorphic

Chemical Composition: sodium aluminosilicate with sulfur and chlorine

Purification: cold water, salt water, incense, sunlight, moonlight, earth

Recharging: quartz cluster, sunlight

Generalities

The ancients appreciated lapis lazuli as a bearer of truth and light. The golden particles on the surface were compared to stars in the night sky. Lapis, also known as a power stone, was one of the most esteemed and widely used stones by the pharaohs of ancient Egypt. It was worn as a protection against the "evil eye" and used as ornaments on royal homes.

Lithotherapy

· Favors the rebirth of our inner divine nature

· Encourages us to face our dark side, illusions, and subconscious repressions so that we may identify with our inner divinity

· Encourages mental force, clarity, and stability, which supports self-healing and contact with the soul

· Inclusions of pyrite and calcite help one to act according to higher ideals and through a more elevated view of oneself

· Purifies the subtle bodies due to inclusions of white calcite

· Facilitates accurate diagnosis during treatment

· Surfaces past traumas, repressed memories, and emotional wounds to be healed and liberated

· Encourages the healthy expression of emotions

· Stimulates communication

· Encourages concentration and mindfulness

· Diminishes anxiety and stress

· Increases physical energy

· Treats eye problems such as cataracts

· Contributes to the proper functioning of the digestive system and the thyroid gland

· Supports one during dizzy spells

LARIMAR

Crystal System: triclinic

Colors: blue, green blue, gray or red with white

Chakras: heart, crown, throat

Hardness: 4.5 to 5

Origin: Dominican Republic

Formation Process: magmatic

Chemical Composition: complex calcaro-sodic silicate

Purification: cold water, incense, sunlight

Recharging: quartz cluster, sunlight

Generalities

Larimar is a feminine power stone that calls upon the energy of "the Goddess," thereby facilitating access to the divine feminine aspect within oneself, whether male or female.

Lithotherapy

· Frees one from self-imposed chains and from slavery to the materialistic world

· Stimulates a more profound understanding of our place in this world

· Dissolves the martyr complex

· Helps us to acknowledge our errors

· Brings peace and honesty

· Develops a capacity to see beyond the point of view of the personality

· Eliminates fear and excessive emotions

· Encourages one to stay calm during dramatic situations

- Stimulates creative and constructive thinking
- Allows one to let events happen without feeling the need to control or manipulate situations
- Motivates self-healing
- Alleviates scalp problems
- Diminishes pain, in particular foot discomforts
- Soothes sore throats
- Dissolves energy blockages in the chest, head, and neck
- Balances and purifies the meridians

LEPIDOLITE

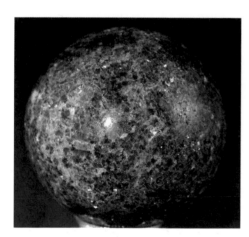

Crystal System: monoclinic

Colors: pink to violet pink, with pearly and translucent luster

Chakras: heart, third eye

Hardness: 2.5 to 3

Origin: Italy, Madagascar, Russia, United States

Formation Process: magmatic

Chemical Composition: complex aluminum, lithium, and potassium aluminosilicate, with fluorine and hydroxyl

Purification: cold water, salt water, incense, minimal sunlight

Recharging: quartz cluster, minimal sunlight

Generalities

Due to the lithium content in its composition, lepidolite is a stone that invites tranquility and balance. It is one of the most powerful stones for soothing strong traumatic emotions, such as anxiety, fear and grief, as well as for calming negative and anxious thoughts.

Lithotherapy

- Favors the elevation of consciousness in overly-materialistic and Cartesian individuals
- Alleviates insomnia
- Offers protection against nightmares
- Calms obsessive thoughts and anxieties
- Offers support for those suffering form bipolar disorders
- Favors autonomy (helps one to fix objectives and to realize them without help from others)
- Protects from outer influences and helps to preserve one's identity in a crowd
- Favors objective evaluation and just decisions
- Motivates one to concentrate on what is essential and to avoid distractions
- Helps to overcome any type of emotional or mental addiction (such as anorexia, drug addictions, etc.)
- Frees and reorganizes psychological models and old behaviors
- Stimulates the intellect and analytical capacities
- Alleviates nervous pains, sciatic nerve pain and other neuralgic or articulation troubles
- Detoxifies and stimulates the purification processes of the skin and of the connective tissues
- Reinforces back muscles
- Strengthens the kidneys and the liver

· Eases the symptoms of epilepsy

· Supports those with Alzheimer's disease

· Alleviates menopausal symptoms

· Eliminates electromagnetic pollution from computers

MAGNESITE

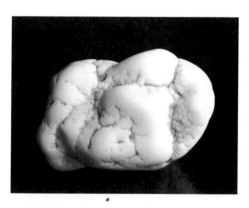

Crystal System: trigonal

Color: creamy white

Chakras: heart, third eye, crown

Hardness: 4 to 4.5

Origin: Austria, Brazil, France, Italy

Formation Process: sedimentary, rarely magmatic

Chemical Composition: magnesium carbonate

Purification: salt water, cold water, sunlight, earth

Recharging: quartz cluster, sunlight

Generalities

Discovered in the thirteenth century, magnesite was called "pure talc." It was later renamed following the discovery of its chemical properties.

Lithotherapy

· Encourages a positive attitude

· Invites self-acceptance and self-love

· Transmits a profound calm

· Tones and stabilizes the mind, balancing the brain hemispheres

· Reduces tension, fear, and irritation

- Balances magnesium deficiencies
- Detoxifies and neutralizes body odor
- Eases spasms and acts as a muscle relaxant
- Soothes headaches and migraines
- Eases symptoms of epilepsy
- Calms menstrual and gastrointestinal cramps
- Treats liver problems
- Slows blood coagulation
- Activates the metabolism of fats and the breakdown of cholesterol
- Prevents the calcification of arteries and tissues
- Acts as a prevention, and support to the treatment, of arteriosclerosis and angina
- Acts as a prophylactic for heart conditions

MAGNETITE

Crystal System: cubic

Color: black metallic, matte

Chakra: root

Hardness: 5.5

Origin: Brazil, Finland, France, Germany, Russia, South Africa, Sweden, United States

Formation Process: magmatic, metamorphic

Chemical Composition: iron oxide, magnetite

Purification: cold water (avoid salt), sunlight, earth

Recharging: quartz cluster, sunlight

Generalities

Magnetite owes its name to the fact that it is a natural magnet. Thanks to this stone, the Chinese were able to invent the magnetic compass, which permitted many adventurous travelers to navigate with greater facility. Without this compass, the history of the world would have no doubt been quite different!

Lithotherapy

- Grounds and anchors one to the physical plane
- Realigns inversed and unbalanced currents of energy within the body and in the earth
- Balances the meridians
- Aligns the chakras and connects them with the nourishing aspects of the earth, which supports the vital force and vigor of the physical-etheric body
- Acts as an energetic shield for the etheric body
- Neutralizes negative emotions such as fear, anger, grief, and excessive attachment
- Balances the mind and the emotions, thereby promoting a strong inner stability
- Prepares and augments one's strength and resistance prior to surgery
- Transmits beneficial energies for regeneration and recovery
- Stimulates and energizes during periods of great fatigue
- Helps to eliminate toxins
- Treats cervical osteoarthritis and bone problems
- Acts as a support to physical traumas
- Eases the symptoms of asthma
- Supports the blood and circulatory system, thereby benefiting cold extremities

- Benefits the skin and hair
- Reduces inflammation and encourages cellular regeneration
- Stops nose bleeds

MALACHITE

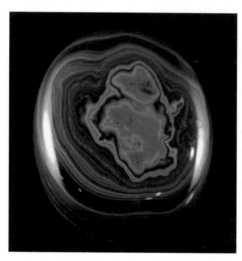

Crystal System: monoclinic

Color: green with black

Chakras: heart, solar plexus

Hardness: 4

Origin: Australia, Chile, Democratic Republic of the Congo, United States, Zimbabwe

Formation Process: sedimentary

Chemical Composition: basic copper carbonate

Purification: cold water, incense, sunlight

Recharging: quartz cluster, sunlight, olive oil (very absorbent, must be cleansed after each use)

Generalities

Malachite has always been associated with femininity, and in many cultures, it was dedicated to the Goddess. It symbolizes the muse of the arts, beauty, curiosity, aesthetics, seduction, and sensuality.

Lithotherapy

- Brings old traumas and negative past experiences to the surface
- Powerfully transforms
- Unerringly indicates what is blocking spiritual growth
- Purifies the physical and emotional bodies

- Acts as a protector from unwanted energies
- Eases anxiety
- Soothes heartache due to breakup
- Facilitates the understanding of complex concepts
- Increases mental powers of observation
- Releases inhibitions and diminishes fears
- Encourages verbal expression
- Develops a sense of beauty, sensuality, friendship, and justice
- Increases the thirst for knowledge
- Encourages one to take risks and to change
- Encourages empathy
- Fights heart diseases and asthma
- Eases pain, fractures, and bruises
- Strengthens the liver and purifies it from toxins
- Benefits the spleen and pancreas
- Eases symptoms of diabetes when worn at the waist level
- Diminishes tissue acidity
- Evacuates excess urea, which causes rheumatism
- Diminishes inflammation and pain caused by arthritis and osteoarthritis
- Rebalances the thyroid and parathyroid glands
- Vibrates to the female sexual organs
- Eases menstrual cramps, acting as an antispasmodic
- Known as the "midwife stone," it facilitates childbirth
- Eases sexual discomfort
- Lowers blood pressure
- Alleviates motion sickness and vertigo

- Strengthens the optic nerves
- Harmonizes DNA and the cellular structure
- Fortifies the immune system
- Favors regeneration
- Protects against radiation
- Absorbs pollutants from the atmosphere as well as the body

In order to benefit from the properties of malachite, it must be in direct contact with the skin. It surfaces and absorbs negative emotions and blockages at the solar plexus, yet it is important to be aware that while malachite will bring all that is repressed to the surface, it will not necessarily appease, dissolve, and heal these emotional wounds. It is therefore recommended to use it in conjunction with another green stone or pink stone such as quartz rose to help with the integrating process. Two or three small clear crystals can also be placed around the malachite to help dissolve what comes forth; this will also keep the stone energized while it works. When placed at the heart, it brings balance and harmony, opening one to unconditional love.

MOLDAVITE

Crystal System: amorphous

Color: green

Chakras: heart, crown, throat, third eye

Hardness: 5.5

Origin: Czech Republic

Formation Process: metamorphic

Chemical Composition: aluminum and silicon oxide

Purification: cold water, incense, moonlight, sunlight

Recharging: quartz cluster, moonlight, sunlight

Generalities

Moldavite was formed when a meteorite impacted the earth's surface 15 million years ago. The violence of the shock itself and the heat produced from it generated a "mix" that was propelled many miles away from the impact zone. This mix settled on the shores of the Vitaya river in the Czech Republic ("Moldau" in German), hence its name.

Lithotherapy

- Grants access to higher spiritual realities due to its significantly elevated vibration
- Redirects the focus to one's main purpose in life, thereby encouraging transformation and expansion of consciousness
- Grants guidance in work, relationships, and lifestyle, thereby promoting loyalty to one's life mission
- Brings understanding to the meaning of life and of humanity's mission here on earth
- Restores harmony and instigates self-healing
- Favors clairvoyance
- Reinforces the capacity for empathy
- Eradicates old, outdated patterns
- Held in the left hand, it guides the therapist in his or her work
- Clears and purifies the meridians
- Inspires creativity and good ideas

Due to the powerful vibration of this stone, it is advisable to use moldavite in moderation for cases of high blood pressure, heart problems, and dizziness. It is also recommended to use it with an effective grounding stone such as jasper in order to remain anchored while working with such high energies. Finally, it is wise to abstain from using moldavite if one experiences strong desires to escape from the realities of the physical plane existence.

MOONSTONE FAMILY

Crystal System: monoclinic

Colors: of the rainbow, white, gray, peach

Chakras: crown, third eye

Hardness: 6 to 6.5

Origin: Australia, India, Madagascar, Myanmar, Sri Lanka, United States

Formation Process: magmatic

Chemical Composition: potassium aluminosilicate

white moonstone

Purification: cold water, salt water, incense, moonlight, sunlight, earth

Recharging: quartz cluster, abundant sunlight and moonlight

Generalities

The name "moonstone" comes from its polished appearance and its blue-white color produced by its thin-layered structure. It is still considered sacred in India.

Lithotherapy

- Inspires softness and sensitivity
- Encourages patience and tolerance
- Awakens the intuition, guiding one to the right action at the right moment
- Balances emotions, thereby promoting clarity
- Guides women to be more balanced in their true feminine expression, with the potential to reveal the nature and power of the Goddess aspect within
- Balances the feminine and masculine polarities in women as well as in men

- Supports one during regression therapy
- Deepens one's meditation practice
- Increases fertility
- Balances hormones and menstrual cycles
- Reduces water retention
- Soothes stomach pains and calms overacidity

Cat Eye Moonstone

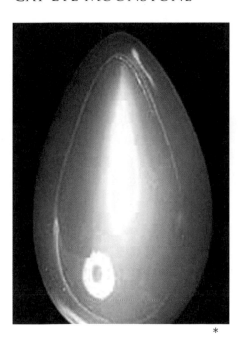

*

Lithotherapy

- Favors clarity of mind and inner vision
- Facilitates concentration when meditating or accessing altered states of consciousness
- Encourages understanding of life lessons and emotional patterns
- Balances the yin and yang polarities
- Supports the central nervous system
- Eases symptoms of asthma
- Diminishes stress
- Treats and protects the liver

New Moonstone

Lithotherapy

· Helps one to see beyond the veil of illusion

· Facilitates journeys into other dimensions

· Holds the power of the new moon, in which everything exists in potentiality

*

Peach Moonstone

Lithotherapy

· Emits a sweet and loving energy, which sustains the heart while stimulating the mind

· Encourages the perception and celebration of the positive aspect of all situations, the divine love that sustains all moments

· Alleviates worry and anxiety by emitting a calming energy that soothes the emotional body

· Encourages sensitivity and intuition in children

RAINBOW MOONSTONE

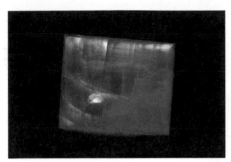

Lithotherapy

· Acts as a prism that shines throughout the whole aura

· Purifies the psychic senses and the mind

· Infuses the auric field with joyful energy

· Encourages clarity when working on intuitive planes

· Provides protection, particularly against psychic attacks, due to its ability to dissipate negative energies before they enter into the energetic field

· Purifies the emotional body and soothes traumas

WHITE MOONSTONE

Lithotherapy

· Represents the power of the moon at its peak

· Stimulates all aspects of psychic perception

· Improves general perception and observation skills

· Contributes to the study of dreams

· May magnify emotional states, as does the full moon itself

· Balances emotions and helps one to be more receptive

Women should avoid using moonstone during the full-moon cycle as it may magnify emotional states.

MORGANITE
(See Pink Beryl)

OBSIDIAN FAMILY

Crystal System: amorphous

Colors: brown, black, glints of silver

Chakra: root

Hardness: 5 to 5.5

Origin: Mexico, United States

Formation Process: magmatic

Chemical Composition: effusion of volcanic rock with glass

Purification: quartz cluster, cold water, incense, moonlight, sunlight

Recharging: quartz cluster, moonlight, sunlight

Generalities

Obsidian ias formed by the rapid cooling of lava, which gives this stone its noncrystallized, amorphous state.

Lithotherapy

· Provides an anchoring link from the root chakra down to the center of the earth

· Purifies the atmosphere of negative influences

· Acts as a shield against psychic attack

· Provides protection for hypersensitive people

· Dissipates fear, shock, and trauma

· Expands consciousness and helps one to change

· Confers mental clarity

· Clears confusion and rigid beliefs

· Sharpens the senses

· Unveils hidden aspects of the unknown

· Attenuates pains and tension and dissolves energy blockages

· Eases vascular constrictions

· Treats trauma to the cellular structure

· Relieves pain in the joints (such as with arthritis) as well as in the muscles

· Reinforces the bloodstream

· Stops hemorrhaging

· Eliminates toxins from the body

· Absorbs environmental pollution

· Has a positive effect on the stomach and bowels

Obsidian acts rapidly and with great force. Its mirroring qualities emphasize truth, thereby helping one to face the darker sides of one's being, such as profound fears, negative traits, and blocked energies. It must therefore always be used with caution and awareness. It may be used with another stone, such as citrine or quartz rose, to help with the integration process, if necessary.

Apache Tear Obsidian

Lithotherapy

· Acts with more moderation than black obsidian

· Gently reveals the darker aspects of our nature

· Anchors and purifies the root chakra

· Eases sadness by revealing its source

· Lightens long-standing grief

· Favors forgiveness

· Pushes away self-imposed limitations

· Increases spontaneity

Golden Obsidian

Lithotherapy

· Guides one to access knowledge pertaining to the future

· Purifies unconstructive aspects of the personality linked to the lower self

· Supports one during inner struggles with one's ego

· Balances the energetic fields

· Stabilizes mood swings

· Treats allergies

*

MAHOGANY OBSIDIAN

Lithotherapy

· Acts with more moderation than black obsidian

· Vibrates with the earth

· Anchors and protects

· Stimulates one's life objective

· Eliminates energy blockages

*   · Facilitates growth in all aspects

· Strengthens the aura

· Restores the normal rotational direction of the hara and solar plexus chakras

· Relieves pain

· Improves circulation

RAINBOW OBSIDIAN

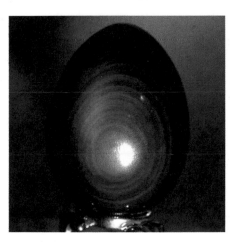

Lithotherapy

· Acts with more moderation than all other obsidian

· Provides powerful protection

· Reveals one's spiritual nature

· Gently removes the "hooks" left in one's aura by a partner

· Absorbs negative energy

· Calms stress and anxiety

Silver Obsidian

Lithotherapy

· Intensifies one's meditation

· Acts as a mirror to one's inner being

· Allows access to purity and humility in the search for truth

· Confers patience and perseverance

*

Snowflake Obsidian

Lithotherapy

· Calms and soothes, thereby encouraging receptivity

· Teaches one to appreciate errors as well as successes

· Instills purity

· Balances the body, the mind, and the spirit

· Favors impartiality and inner poise

ONYX

Crystal System: trigonal

Color: black

Chakra: root

Hardness: 6.5 to 7

Origin: Brazil, Madagascar

Formation Process: magmatic

Chemical Composition: silicon oxide

Purification: cold water, salt water, incense, moonlight, sunlight, earth

Recharging: quartz cluster, moonlight, sunlight

Generalities

During the Middle Ages, onyx was seen as an instigator of conflict and discord. Nowadays, it is said that wearing it for an extended period may cause listlessness and melancholy. Onyx is a black variety of agate. Pregnant women should avoid using it.

Lithotherapy

- Increases concentration and revives the memory
- Refines judgment, allowing one to make better decisions
- Stimulates analytical thinking and logic
- Encourages humility
- Inspires studiousness and self-control
- Confers a sense of responsibility
- Gives support to people who are too easily influenced, thereby helping them to reach their true objectives

- Grounds and anchors

- Absorbs negativity while letting through positive vibrations

- Protects against accidents

- Balances the yin and yang energies

- Helps one to accept conflict

- Treats inner-ear conditions

- Improves eyesight

- Reinforces the immune system and protects against risks of infection

- Improves the condition of the skin, nails, and hair

- Strengthens the heart

- Treats ulcers

- Improves the functioning of the sensory and motor nerves

OPAL FAMILY

Crystal System: amorphous

Colors: see specific types

Chakras: according to type

Hardness: 5.5 to 6.5

Origin: Australia, Brazil, Guatemala, Japan, Mexico, Peru, United States

Formation Process: sedimentary, magmatic for the fire opal

Chemical Composition: hydrated silicon oxide

Noble opal

Purification: quartz cluster, a lot of water, incense, moonlight, sunlight, earth

Recharging: Quartz cluster, water, moonlight, sunlight; rub the opal gently with a high-quality vegetable oil once a month, as this will nourish it and help prevent dehydration

Generalities

Opal's reputation demands respect because it is known to carry the power to bring luck or to take it away. Its high percentage of water (up to 20 percent) makes it a tool that can soothe or amplify emotions. It must therefore always be worn with an awareness of its potential and with a certainty of its positive effects. In case of doubt, refrain from wearing it.

BLACK OPAL (1st AND 7th CHAKRAS)

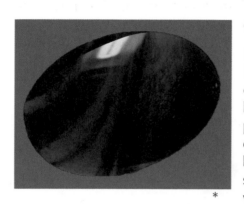

*

Generalities

Using a black opal in lithotherapy first requires determining the intentions behind the desire to use it, particularly if they are linked to emotions. It is worth noting that black opal, a very powerful stone, can support positive as well as negative intentions. One must always remain aware and in control of one's thoughts and emotions while working with this stone; benevolent intentions are a must. Here's a proverb linked to the black opal: "Beware of what you ask for; you might actually get it."

Lithotherapy

- A stone of mystery and magic
- Stimulates the root chakra and links it with the crown chakra
- Helps to integrate one's spiritual aspirations to everyday life
- Strongly amplifies intent
- Contains the power of manifestation when the will is linked to a precise goal

- Supports those who have undertaken profound inner work
- Favors letting go of negative experiences that create certain karmic patterns
- Frees one from traumatic memories governing certain periods of life (it is helpful to have the help of an experienced guide for this work)
- Supports one when facing the darkest fears
- Helps to overcome phobias and panic attacks
- Makes it possible to visit the dark aspects of being while staying connected to the light
- Supports those who help lost souls by directing them toward more-luminous worlds
- Contributes to diminishing tumors and cysts

FIRE OPAL (1st CHAKRA, YELLOW ORANGE TO FLUORESCENT RED)

Lithotherapy

- Reinforces personal power
- Awakens the inner fire
- Protects from danger
- Encourages a spontaneous and impulsive character
- Inspires risk taking
- Gives hope

*

- Awakens one to the joy of being alive
- Stimulates the libido, as it acts on the sexual chakra
- Transforms sexuality into spontaneous pleasure
- Allows one to quickly seize reality and to act accordingly
- Helps one to overcome emotional problems caused by mistreatment and injustice
- Frees one from the past and from the risk of discordant behaviors caused by strong, recurring emotional patterns

- Clears up feelings of sadness stemming from the present and past lives

- Contributes to the proper functioning of the kidneys and adrenal glands (such as production of adrenaline)

- Prevents exhaustion

- Fortifies blood circulation

- Aids digestion

- Soothes menstrual pains caused by hormonal imbalances

HYDROPHANE OPAL (1st CHAKRA)

Lithotherapy

- Contributes to the exteriorization of certain qualities repressed due to lack of self-confidence

- Stabilizes moods

- Supports one during out-of-body transitions

- Teaches that the body is a temporary vehicle for the soul

*

NOBLE OPAL (7th CHAKRA; MILKY WHITE WITH MULTICOLOR IRIDESCENCE)

Lithotherapy

- Symbolizes purity in sentiments, fidelity, shared confidences, and loving-kindness

- Favors sleep

White Opal (4th chakra)

Lithotherapy

· Stimulates originality and dynamic creativity

· Alleviates worries, chronic stress, and depression

· Communicates the joy of living on earth

· Reinforces the will to live

· Brings mental clarity and spontaneity

· Soothes emotions and encourages a positive attitude

· Is associated with love, passion, desire, and eroticism

· Comforts those who have lived through abuses of all kinds

· Fights exhaustion

· Revives the memory

· Contributes to the treatment of Parkinson's disease

· Fights infections and fever

· Regulates insulin levels

· Eases symptoms of premenstrual syndrome

· Reinforces eyesight when taken as an elixir

PERIDOT (OLIVINE OR CHRYSOLITE)

Crystal System: rhombic

Colors: from pale green to yellowish green to olive green

Chakras: heart, solar plexus

Hardness: 6.5 to 7

Origin: Australia, Brazil, Congo, Island of Zerbiget (Red Sea), Myanmar, Norway, South Africa, United States

Formation Process: magmatic

Chemical Composition: iron and magnesium silicate

Purification: cold water, salt water, incense, sunlight, earth (rarely necessary, for peridot is very resistant to negative energies)

Recharging: quartz cluster, sunlight

Generalities

Peridot, or olivine, is a protective stone and a symbol of the olive tree and olive oil, which are recognized for their nourishing and purifying aspects.

Lithotherapy

· Facilitates understanding of the necessity for change and growth

· Reveals negative habits hindering one from reaching what is necessary to evolve

· Stimulates and purifies the solar plexus and the heart, bringing openness and acceptance

· Contributes to regulating the cycles of life in the physical, emotional, and mental bodies

- Protects against outside influences and prevents them from affecting one's balance
- Helps heal injured egos by attenuating anger, resentment, envy and jealousy
- Inspires one to be happy and to rejoice in the unique expression of one's own life
- Increases energy
- Harmonizes and balances emotions
- Stimulates the mind
- Attracts wisdom and friendship
- Provides freedom from self-reproach
- Increases confidence and assurance without awakening aggressiveness
- Encourages self-forgiveness and the acceptance of personal faults
- Diminishes stress
- Purifies the subtle bodies and the mind
- Reinforces the etheric body
- Eliminates toxins from the body
- Stimulates the liver and bile production
- Activates the metabolism (tonic effect)
- Provides relief of skin ailments, especially warts
- Facilitates proper functioning of the intestines
- Reinforces the heart, thymus, and lungs
- Treats the gallbladder and spleen
- Facilitates childbirth by strengthening muscular contractions and by diminishing pain when placed on the abdomen

PETRIFIED WOOD (XYLOÏDE)

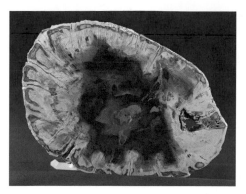

Crystal System: trigonal or amorphous

Colors: brown, yellow, reddish

Chakras: solar plexus, root

Hardness: 7

Origin: Argentina, Egypt, United States (Arizona)

Formation Process: sedimentary

Chemical Composition: silicon oxide

Purification: cold water, incense, sunlight

Recharging: quartz cluster, abundant sunlight

Generalities

Petrified wood is about 200 million years old and dates back to the first conifer tree, Araucaria, from the Jurassic period.

Lithotherapy

· Encourages trust in the rhythm of life and in what is needed to evolve

· Guides slowly but surely toward spiritual transformation

· Gives the impression of being at the right place at the right moment

· Stimulates inner images and past lives

· Helps to recognize and to release emotional patterns transmitted from one's family history

· Relaxes, calms, and encourages, making time for reflection and contemplation

· Grounds and anchors

- Facilitates the creation of a positive environment
- Encourages one to live simply
- Acts as a link to the earth and its energy
- Communicates a feeling of being at home here on earth
- Calms the nerves
- Confers a feeling of well-being
- Diminishes preoccupations and grants strength to sort through irritating details
- Revives the memory and gives support to distracted people
- Excels against all kinds of physical problems
- Activates the metabolism
- Favors the physical and intellectual growth of children
- Supports one in the case of excess weight (often caused by a lack of connection to the earth)
- Reinforces bone structure and treats broken bones
- Offers protection against intestinal parasites
- Purifies the liver and the blood
- Balances the liver and the gallbladder
- Treats the hair when taken as an elixir

PIETERSITE (TEMPEST STONE)

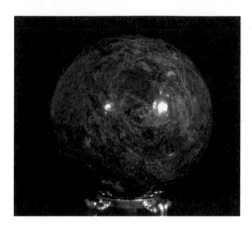

Crystal System: trigonal

Colors: golden brown to blue gray with black traces

Chakras: throat, heart, solar plexus, third eye

Hardness: 7

Origin: Namibia, South Africa

Formation Process: magmatic

Chemical Composition: see tiger eye, hawk eye, and jasper

Purification: cold water, distilled salt water, incense, moonlight, sunlight, earth

Recharging: quartz cluster, moonlight, sunlight

Generalities

The discovery of this stone is relatively recent. It is composed of jasper, hawk eye, tiger eye, and possibly onyx.

Lithotherapy

· Stimulates intuition and extrasensory faculties

· Connects the day-to-day consciousness to the spiritual consciousness

· Anchors the etheric body to the physical body

· Stimulates the third eye

· Favors subtle spiritual visions

· Dispels spiritual illusions

· Fortifies and engenders a positive attitude

· Supports one during chaotic situations

- The golden brown variety eases suicidal tendencies and depression
- Encourages mastery over charged memories and unresolved inner conflicts
- Inspires impeccability in times of rapid and boisterous change (personal or collective) and the creation of a new order from chaos
- Offers the opportunity to remain focused and contemplative in the midst of distractions
- Allows one to keep a certain distance without becoming indifferent
- Opens the mind to original ideas
- Invigorates the mind
- Facilitates communication and stimulates eloquence
- Releases one from deep-rooted habits
- Eliminates mental and verbal conditioning (imposed by authority figures)
- Dispels blockages caused by an overly stubborn attitude
- Helps to distinguish truth from falsehood
- Encourages the ability to stay loyal to principles
- Leads one to speak out and to explore all that can block the way to the truth
- Activates an understanding of impressions and helps to keep the mind in a receptive state
- Purifies and energizes the meridians
- Fights illnesses caused by stress, anxiety, and burnout
- Provides the necessary resistance to avoid professional burnout
- Supports the lungs and treats respiratory ailments
- Balances hormones
- Stimulates the pituitary gland (hypophysis), thereby balancing the endocrine system, which stimulates hormone production that governs metabolism, blood pressure, growth, sexuality, and body temperature

- Helps with hearing disorders and tinnitus
- Treats and clears vocal cords
- Harmonizes digestive functions, especially the liver and intestines
- Facilitates the assimilation of essential nutrients in food
- Benefits the legs and feet
- Provides relief during chronic illness

PREHNITE

Crystal System: rhombic

Colors: yellow, light green to yellowish green

Chakras: heart, solar plexus, third eye

Hardness: 6 to 6.5

Origin: Australia, China, Scotland, South Africa, United States

Formation process: magmatic

Chemical Composition: sodium and calcium silicate

Purification: cold water, incense, sunlight, earth

Recharging: quartz cluster, sunlight

Generalities

Prehnite is said to be a stone of unconditional love that will "heal the healer." Meditating with it allows one to connect to the energetic framework of the universe. It establishes a link with the archangel Raphael and facilitates a connection to other spiritual and extraterrestrial beings.

Lithotherapy

- Increases psychic abilities and intuition
- Enhances the visualization process and motivates one toward deep meditation in which the higher self can be contacted
- Pinpoints the way to spiritual evolution
- Prepares one for any eventuality
- Favors a tranquil environment that brings peace and protection
- Seals the aura with a protective shield of divine energy
- Teaches how to be in harmony with nature and the elements
- Helps to eliminate what is no longer useful to personal growth, whether it be possessions or ties with others
- Contributes to dissolving escape and repression mechanisms
- Supports one when facing repressed memories and the associated liberation of emotions
- Increases the capacity to receive
- Alleviates phobias, nightmares, and deep fears
- Favors understanding by analysis
- Speeds up the processing of sensory information
- Facilitates the discovery of the root cause of certain problems or illnesses
- Activates the metabolism
- Stimulates all renewal processes in the body
- Speeds up the elimination of toxins accumulated in body fat
- Helps with urinary incontinence by treating the kidneys and bladder
- Treats thymus, shoulder, breast, and lung problems

PROPHECY STONE

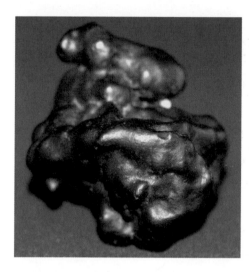

Crystal System: unavailable

Color: metallic brown

Chakras: crown, root, third eye

Hardness: unknown

Origin: Libya

Formation process: sedimentary

Chemical Composition: unknown (contains iron)

Purification: quartz cluster, incense

Recharging: quartz cluster (very little recharging necessary)

Generalities

The prophecy stone is a concretion that contains a considerable amount of compact material around a nucleus. Its exterior color and texture cause people to suspect that it is in fact a meteorite. Its chemical composition is still unknown, although iron has been detected. Its name derives from prophetic visions that have been obtained while meditating with it.

Lithotherapy

· Allows energy to descend from the crown chakra to fill the entire body

· Anchors the light body to the physical body

· Potentially catalyzes visions of the future via meditation

· Harmonizes earth and celestial energies

· Anchors one to the physical while exploring altered states of consciousness

- Stabilizes high-frequency energies to be integrated in the physical
- Helps to expel toxins from the cells
- Supports the body during chemotherapy and radiotherapy treatments

PYRITE

Crystal System: cubic

Color: golden yellow

Chakras: solar plexus, third eye

Hardness: 6 to 6.5

Origin: Italy, Peru, Spain

Formation process: magmatic, metamorphic, sedimentary

Chemical Composition: iron bisulfure

Purification: cold water, incense, sunlight, earth

Recharging: quartz cluster, sunlight

Generalities

Pyrite has been called "fire stone" for its ability to produce sparks when hit. Magical properties have been attributed to it due to the fire that is believed to inhabit its form. It is also called "fool's gold," as it is has often been confused with gold.

Lithotherapy

- Acts as an energetic shield that clears negative energy or pollutants, including infectious disease
- Favors self-knowledge
- Opens the door to possible and necessary changes

- Helps one to reveal and to confront the dark and luminous aspects of one's nature
- Illuminates hidden secrets and memories, thereby encouraging greater openness and honesty
- Reinforces self-confidence and feelings of virility (it may be too powerful for some personality types, who may become aggressive)
- Eliminates inertia and feelings of mediocrity
- Diminishes feelings of inferiority and the tendency to be overly-submissive
- Alleviates melancholy and intense despair
- Stimulates the circulation of ideas
- Encourages organization, structure, and order
- Allows one to draw from personal talents and potential
- Useful for the creation of commercial strategies
- Teaches how to see beyond appearances and is therefore helpful during diplomatic work
- Stimulates mental activity by bringing greater blood flow to the head
- Stimulates memory
- Enlarges and structures mental capacity, balancing instinct with intuition and creativity with analysis
- Aligns the meridians
- Increases energy and helps one to overcome fatigue
- Blocks energy leaks in the subtle bodies
- Increases oxygen in the blood and fortifies the circulatory system
- Stimulates cell formation and repairs damaged DNA
- Fortifies the digestive tract and neutralizes ingested toxins
- Soothes sleep disruption due to stomach ailments
- Overcomes problems caused by asthma and bronchitis

In past civilizations, people wore pyrite amulets for their healing properties.

It is recommended to avoid wearing this stone for extended periods. It produces a black ferrous sulphide deposit when mixed with perspiration, which can irritate the skin. It is better to use this stone in meditation, during supervised treatments, or to wear it in a location where it can be checked regularly. When worn around the neck, pyrite protects the physical and subtle bodies and neutralizes malevolent energies and dangers.

RHODOCHROSITE

Crystal System: trigonal

Colors: pale pink to dark pink

Chakras: heart, solar plexus

Hardness: 4

Origin: Argentina, Russia, South Africa, United States, Uruguay

Formation Process: sedimentary

Chemical Composition: manganese carbonate

Purification: cold water, incense, sunlight (frequent purification is recommended)

Recharging: quartz cluster, sunlight

Generalities

The name "rhodochrosite" comes from the Greek word "rhodon" which signifies "rose." Rhodochrosite is considered to be a stone of altruistic love and compassion.

Lithotherapy

- Possesses a particular affinity with the heart chakra
- Awakens universal love
- Attracts one's soul mate
- Alleviates stress and emotional turmoil
- Encourages greater mastery over the emotions
- Facilitates emotional healing in cases of sexual abuse
- Due to its overall calming effect, it promotes greater ease of movement and facilitates the breathing process
- Alleviates symptoms of depression
- Confers a positive attitude and enthusiasm towards life
- Consoles those who feel unloved
- Encourages spontaneity and emotional expression
- Revives the memory
- Stimulates creativity and innovation
- Awakens, stimulates, and motivates one to take action
- Confers the courage to face fears
- Improves the awareness of personal worth
- Relieves gastric ulcers
- Purifies the blood and stimulates blood circulation
- Restores the elasticity in blood vessels, thereby regulating blood pressure and relieving migraines
- Invigorates sexual activity by revitalizing the sexual organs
- Fights osteoarthritis
- Fortifies the heart by diminishing palpitations
- Treats skin allergies
- Balances the thyroid gland

· Relieves kidney and intestinal problems

· Absorbs the irritants that can be found in the respiratory tract, thus alleviating asthma and other breathing difficulties

· Improves vision

Rhodochrosite can be placed directly on the body, the wrist, the heart, or the solar plexus.

RHODONITE

Crystal System: triclinic

Colors: pink, mottled red or black

Chakra: heart

Hardness: 5.5 to 6.5

Origin: Australia, Canada, India, Madagascar, Mexico, Russia, South Africa, Sweden, United States

Formation Process: metamorphic

Chemical Composition: mangano-calcareous silicate

Purification: cold water, incense, sunlight, earth

Recharging: quartz cluster, sunlight

Generalities

As with other pink stones, rhodonite emanates the energy of unconditional love. Like her cousin rhodochrosite, rhodonite encourages loving without separative barriers, always for the benefit of those who cross our paths.

Lithotherapy

· Confers emotional balance

· Balances the yin and yang

· Stimulates, liberates, and activates the heart chakra

· Encourages unity and brotherhood

· Heals self-destructive emotions as well as deep-rooted emotional wounds

· Dissolves resentment, anger, and suffering caused by abuse, betrayal and abandonment

· Encourages forgiveness and neutralizes vengeance

· Allows one to see the solution to seemingly insoluble problems, hence giving more meaning to life

· Spurs insightfulness during conflicts (often caused by a lack of self-love)

· Encourages attention to details in relationships

· Diminishes the impact of emotional shock, and dissipates panic attacks

· Relieves wounds and insect bites

· Helps prevent scarring

· Treats arthritis

· Soothes stomach ulcers

· Treats emphysema and streptococcal infections of the throat

· Eases the symptoms of multiple sclerosis

· Alleviates hearing problems

· Reinforces the immune system

· Stimulates fertility in both males and females

Rhodonite's numerous physical and emotional benefits have granted it the reputation of being an essential "first aid" stone and therefore a useful addition to first aid kits.

ROSE QUARTZ

Crystal System: trigonal

Colors: pale pink to dark pink

Chakra: heart

Hardness: 7

Origin: Brazil, Madagascar, United States (Arkansas)

Formation Process: magmatic

Chemical Composition: silicon and manganese oxide

Purification: cold water, salt water, incense, sunlight, earth

Recharging: quartz cluster, sunlight

Generalities

Rose quartz is the stone of unconditional love and inner peace.

Lithotherapy

- Harmonizes with the heart chakra
- Transmits unconditional love for oneself and for others
- Supports one in moments of emotional shock
- Soothes emotional pain and heartache by reinforcing self-love and acceptance, thereby reinforcing the capacity to love others
- Encourages forgiveness and trust
- Helps to counter depression
- Confers gentleness, infinite tenderness, absolute calm, and a connection to one's spiritual self
- Inspires harmony in chaotic situations

· Calms worries and preoccupations

· Enhances discernment

· Favors service, openness to others and to life, as well as the desire to create favorable surroundings

· Balances all the systems in the body

· Strengthens the heart

· Reinforces the sexual organs

· Increases fertility

· Treats the kidneys and adrenal glands

· Attenuates vertigo

· Eliminates impurities from bodily fluids

· Relieves insomnia

· Assists individuals affected by Alzheimer's, Parkinson's, or senile dementia

· Relieves arthritis pain

· Soothes burns

· Helps to maintain a satin-like complexion

· Protects against television and computer radiation (electromagnetic frequencies)

RUBY

Crystal System: trigonal

Color: red

Chakra: root

Hardness: 9

Origin: Brazil, Cambodia, Myanmar, India, Kenya, Madagascar, Mexico, Russia, Sri Lanka, Thailand

Formation Process: magmatic, metamorphic

Chemical Composition: aluminum and chrome oxide

Purification: cold water, salt water, incense, sunlight, earth

Recharging: quartz cluster, abundant sunlight

Generalities

Ruby is endowed with one of the most powerful vibrations of the mineral kingdom. According to an ancient Burmese legend, inserting a ruby under the skin could render a man invincible. The ruby was for a long time and by many cultures considered a stone of power and royalty.

Lithotherapy

- Instills energy, balance, and dynamism
- Awakens enthusiasm
- Confers vigor and passion for life
- Increases motivation
- Encourages the establishment of realistic goals
- Stimulates and balances the heart chakra
- Constitutes a powerful shield against psychic attacks and against "vampires" of the heart energy
- Facilitates positive dreaming and visualization
- Grants long-lasting wealth and passion (stone of abundance)
- Unveils anger and negativity so that it can be resolved
- Encourages dynamic leadership
- Instills a positive and courageous state of mind
- Offers a strong inner stability during debates and conflictual situations
- Activates the pineal gland
- Stimulates the libido
- Calms hyperactivity
- Fortifies the immune system
- Detoxifies the blood, the body, and the lymphatic system

Rutile

Crystal System: quadratic

Colors: dark gray with metallic shine, generally gilded and occasionally orange red

Chakras: crown, root

Hardness: 6 to 6.5

Origin: Brazil, Madagascar, United States (Arkansas)

Formation Process: magmatic

Chemical Composition: titanium oxide

Purification: cold water, salt water, incense, sunlight, earth

Recharging: quartz cluster, abundance of sunlight

Generalities

Rutile acts as an antenna that can be synchronized to divine frequencies. Thus, it not only enhances psychic abilities, but also amplifies emotions whether they are positive or negative.

Lithotherapy

· Inspires hope

· Encourages integrity, truthfulness, and independence

· Confers a noble spirit

· Enlarges the vision and broadens the mind

· Stabilizes the emotions

· Acts as an antidepressant by uplifting the spirits

· Dissipates hidden and buried fears

· Encourages the adoption of a new and more positive lifestyle

- Protects against psychic attacks
- Balances the thyroid gland
- Relieves breathing problems and chronic bronchitis
- Activates the process of cellular regeneration
- Stimulates physical growth as well as the proper flow of energy in the body
- Treats impotence

SAPPHIRE

Crystal System: trigonal

Colors: blue, colorless, yellow, black

Chakras: throat, third eye

Hardness: 9

Origin: Australia, Brazil, Czech Republic, India, Kenya, Sri Lanka

Formation Process: magmatic, metamorphic

Chemical Composition: aluminum, iron and titanium oxide

Purification: cold water, salt water, incense, moonlight, earth

Recharging: quartz cluster, moonlight

Generalities

The word "sapphire" draws its name from the Sanskrit word "sani" that signifies "Saturn," hence, the ancients from India and Europe had identified it as the stone of Saturn. The sapphire is also acknowledged as a stone of wisdom, as it favors the desire for knowledge.

Lithotherapy

- Helps to wisely evaluate one's life
- Known as the stone of prosperity, it attracts gifts and blessings
- Awakens faith and love for the truth
- Calms the mind and repels intrusive thoughts
- Promotes objectivity and an analytical mind
- Enhances the power of intention and the will, in order to encourage the rapid manifestation of ideas and thoughts
- Invites peace and inner serenity
- Aligns the physical, mental, and spiritual bodies, conferring a better balance
- Dissipates spiritual confusion
- Stimulates concentration
- Diminishes frustration
- Facilitates self-expression
- Fights depression
- Relieves psychological illnesses
- Calms hallucinations
- Encourages the will to heal
- Regularizes the functioning of the glands
- Calms overactive physiological systems
- Relieves eye troubles
- Aids the circulatory system, treats illnesses of the blood, and calms hemorrhages
- Improves the elasticity of the veins and strengthens them
- Reduces fever
- Supports the intestines
- Assists with problems of the nervous system (brain and nerves)
- Benefits the vagus nerve

SELENITE FAMILY

Crystal System: monoclinic

Colors: beige, brown white, pink, transparent (rare, gem quality) greenish

Chakras: according to color

Hardness: 2

Origin: France, Great Britain, Greece, Mexico, Poland, Russia, United States

Formation Process: sedimentary

Chemical Composition: hydrated calcium sulfate

Purification: incense, abundance of sunlight, avoid water and salt

Recharging: quartz cluster, frequent and abundant sunlight

Generalities

Placing a significant piece of selenite in a house will ensure a serene atmosphere. Selenite also acts as a protective stone when a piece is placed in the corner of each room.

Lithotherapy

- Enhances telepathy due to its purity
- Aligns all the bodies
- Relaxes and clarifies the mind
- Encourages expansion of consciousness
- Anchors the body of light on earth
- Instills a deep sense of peace (meditation stone)

- Allows one to contact past and future lives
- Helps one develops intuition and discernment
- Eliminates disorientation
- Allows one to perceive subtleties
- Brings a conscious understanding to the unconscious
- Activates and stimulates the memory and intellect
- Improves concentration and clarity of mind
- Generates a sense of physical well-being
- Produces a positive effect on the brain
- Soothes the nervous system and eases spasms
- Aligns the spine
- Confers flexibility
- Eases symptoms of epilepsy
- Neutralizes mercury poisoning caused by dental fillings
- Strengthens bones and teeth
- Benefits the stomach
- Strengthens body tissues and restores the skin's elasticity
- Stimulates cellular regeneration, which may prolong life
- Benefits the prostate
- Fortifies the uterus and supports the organs of the abdomen during pregnancy
- Supports during breast-feeding

It is preferable to avoid placing selenite in water or in a humid environment, for it tends to dissolve in such conditions.

Blue Selenite

*

Lithotherapy

· Calms the mind when placed on the third eye

· Allows one to ignore mental chatter during meditation

· Rapidly reveals the root of a problem

Desert Rose Selenite

Lithotherapy

· Allows to disengage one from persistent, self-imposed programming

· Reinforces affirmations relating to specific goals

Fishtail Selenite

Lithotherapy

· Soothes and stabilizes the emotions

· Dissolves tension

· Facilitates contact with the angelic realm

· Treats illnesses of the nervous system

GREEN SELENITE

*

Lithotherapy

· Motivates one to act for the greater good

· Encourages self-acceptance

· Acts as prevention against ageing of the skin and skeletal system

ORANGE BROWN SELENITE

*

Lithotherapy

· Anchors angelic energies

· Contributes to the healing of the earth

SERAPHINITE

Crystal System: monoclinic

Colors: green with a silver gleam, occasionally white, brown, yellow, red

Chakras: all

Hardness: 4

Origin: Russia

Formation Process: unknown

Chemical Composition: silicon, oxygen, hydrogen, aluminum, magnesium, iron

Purification: green clay, cold water, sunlight

Recharging: quartz cluster, sunlight

Generalities

As its name suggests, seraphinite resonates with the order of angels closest to God and most luminous, the Seraphs. Seraphin signifies "the one who sets ablaze," and who purifies using the divine flame and lightning. It is said that seraphinite is an essential healing stone in this new era. It is also considered the stone of angels due to its elevated vibration.

Lithotherapy

· Amplifies the beneficial properties of other stones

· Inspires the desire to live consciously and to develop intuition

· Protects, especially the heart chakra

· Purifies the two principal energy channels, Ida and Pingala

· Balances the yin and yang

· Facilitates the opening of the heart and crown chakra

· Encourages transformation and transmutation

- Powerfully regenerates and strengthens
- Fights addictions
- Acts against the growth and reproduction of cancer cells
- Reduces chills
- Supports the nerves and brain cells
- Purifies the blood and eliminates toxins in the kidneys and liver
- Contributes to weight loss

Note that when placed at the crown chakra, seraphinite balances and aligns all the chakras.

SERPENTINE

Crystal System: monoclinic

Colors: pale green to yellowish green

Chakras: heart, throat

Hardness: 2.5 to 4

Origin: Afghanistan, Alps (the), Armorican and Central Massif, China, England, Italy, New Zealand, Norway, Pyrenees, Russia, South Africa, United States, Zimbabwe

Formation Process: metamorphic

Chemical Composition: basic magnesium silicate

Purification: cold water, incense, earth

Recharging: quartz cluster, earth, avoid sunlight

Generalities

In ancient Assyria, serpentine was worn to attract benedictions from gods and goddesses. It was also used to repel illness and counter witchcraft.

Lithotherapy

- Balances mood swings
- Directs a curative energy towards mental and emotional imbalances
- Conveys a peaceful attitude in the midst of conflict, thereby promoting constructive solutions
- Appeases nervousness and stress
- Instills a sense of mastery over one's life
- Communicates peace and gentleness to the emotional body thereby encouraging the release of the fear of change and adversity
- Grounds during meditation and spiritual exploration
- Stimulates visualization during meditative exercises
- Fortifies the heart and lungs
- Soothes headaches
- Favors calcium and magnesium absorption
- Strengthens the kidneys, bladder, stomach, and intestines
- Calms cramps and eases menstrual pains
- Treats hypoglycemia and diabetes
- Re-energizes
- Protects while traveling

SMITHSONITE (BONAMITE)

Crystal System: trigonal

Colors: white to gray, lavender, purple, pink, green to blue, brown, yellow

Chakras: according to color.

Hardness: 5

Origin: Greece, Italy, Mexico, Namibia, Spain, United States

Formation Process: sedimentary

Chemical Composition: zinc carbonate

Purification: cold water

Recharging: moonlight

Generalities

It is said that the vibration of smithsonite resonates with Quan Yin, the feminine bodhisattva of compassion. Quan Yin is frequently called upon for her healing qualities, as well as her capacity to dissolve interpersonal conflicts and relationship problems. Smithsonite is a stone of absolute gentleness that eases feelings of loneliness. Wearing smithsonite is somewhat like having a compassionate friend by one's side.

Lithotherapy

· Stimulates the understanding of universal love
· Contributes to re-establishing the awareness of the Unity of the Whole
· Encourages profound relaxation, thereby calming the mind and instilling a deeper meditative state
· Enhances sensitivity to subtle energies emanating from other dimensions
· Accentuates psychic powers, telepathic communication, and conversation with beings of the angelic realm

- Activates the heart through the crown chakra inspiring a greater comprehension of emotions
- Liberates one from feelings of grief and soothes broken hearts
- Is an important emotional healer that calms anger and resentment
- Allows one to see the brighter side, even in moments of depression
- Is beneficial for those or who feel unloved or unwanted, or who have had a difficult childhood experience
- Heals the inner child, alleviating the negative effects of abuse and psychological neglect
- Favors gentleness, stimulates compassion, and encourages one to support others
- Facilitates friendship by encouraging inner harmony and harmony with others
- Confers courage
- Contributes to dissolving negative energies and blockages in the energy fields
- Forms a protective shield against unnecessary obstacles
- Provides relief from mental exhaustion and intense stress
- Supports those who suffer from alcoholism
- Treats osteoporosis
- Regulates weight
- Augments physical energy
- Aids the reproductive organs
- Balances the endocrine system
- Benefits the sinuses
- Helps with digestive problems
- Restores elasticity to the veins and muscles
- Strongly supports the immune system

The bond between client and therapist may be greatly improved during a lithotherapy session when both wear smithsonite. This may also enhance the connection to their respective guides.

SODALITE

Crystal System: cubic

Color: blue with black and white inclusions

Chakras: throat, third eye

Hardness: 5.5 to 6

Origin: Africa, Brazil, Canada, India

Formation Process: magmatic

Chemical Composition: complex sodium and chlorine aluminosilicate

Purification: cold water, incense, moonlight, earth

Recharging: quartz cluster, moonlight

Generalities

In Africa, sodalite is considered to be a stone of protection. The Celts and Greeks honored sodalite as a prophecy stone, while the Christians believed it enhanced perception.

Lithotherapy

· Aligns the superior chakras

· Contributes to awakening the third eye

· Confers humility and courage

· Builds true confidence, thus reducing the need for excessive praise for personal merits

· Encourages healthy idealism

· Instigates the search for the truth

· Inspires fidelity toward oneself and one's convictions

· Transforms the defensive or hypersensitive personality by helping the heart to release fear, guilt, and control mechanisms, which prevent one from being authentic

- Increases self-respect and reveals obscure aspects of the self, to be accepted in a nonjudgmental manner
- Helps to balance and eventually master the emotions
- Enhances intuitive perception and facilitates the verbal expression of feelings
- Calms anxiety and panic attacks
- Invites one to let go of obsolete and rigid mental conditioning, hence creating an opening for new possibilities
- Encourages objectivity
- Stimulates the brain and logical thinking
- Purifies the mind
- Prepares the mind for intuitive knowledge and introspection
- Supports group work, stimulating confidence, camaraderie, harmony and solidarity, as well as contributing to materializing ideas and goals
- Protects the physical body and the psyche (with surface irridations)
- Activates the pineal gland
- Cleanses the organs and lymphatic system
- Activates the immune system
- Balances the metabolism
- Prevents calcium deficiency
- Counteracts the emission of electromagnetic pollution (computers, etc.)
- Fights damage caused by radiation
- Treats the throat, the vocal cords, the larynx, and cases of persistent hoarseness
- Relieves digestive problems
- Reduces fever and blood pressure
- Stimulates fluid absorption in the body

Sodalite is most beneficial when placed directly on the skin, at the wrist, heart, throat, third eye, or solar plexus.

Sugilite (Luvulite or Royal Azel)

Crystal System: hexagonal

Colors: black, violet, translucent

Chakras: all

Hardness: 6.5 to 7

Origin: Japan, South Africa

Formation Process: magmatic

Chemical Composition: aluminum complex, manganese and iron silicate, with lithium and potassium

Purification: cold water, salt water, incense, sunlight, earth

Recharging: quartz cluster, sunlight

Generalities

Only two deposits of sugilite have been discovered to this day, the first being in 1944, which makes it a rare stone. Its therapeutic properties were recognized in 1980, when it was then renowned as a New Age stone, a symbol of the Aquarius era, bringing to earth the numerous benefits of the violet ray.

Translucent sugilite purifies the lymphatic system and the blood. It is placed at the third eye to ease headaches and to diminish despair.

Lithotherapy

· Opens and aligns all the chakras concerned with spiritual love

· Inspires the expansion of consciousness

· Encourages living according to one's truth

· Eases psychic tensions, paranoia, and symptoms of schizophrenia

- Alleviates sorrow, sadness, and fear by inspiring self-forgiveness
- Favors forgiveness by eliminating hostility
- Assists with conflict resolution
- Inspires finding solutions that answer to everyone's needs
- Contributes to constructive group work
- Encourages affectionate communication
- Surmounts learning difficulties such as dyslexia
- Soothes the nerves and brain
- Reduces intense pain and treats headaches
- Is beneficial for epilepsy and motor problems
- Eases symptoms of autism

SUNSTONE

Crystal System: triclinic

Colors: brown, orange, peach, pink, red with shimmering inclusions of goethite or hematite

Chakras: throat, hara, solar plexus, root

Hardness: 6 to 6.5

Origin: Canada, India, Norway, Russia, United States

Formation process: magmatic

Chemical Composition: sodium and calcium aluminosilicate

Purification: cold water, incense, sunlight, earth

Recharging: quartz cluster, sunlight

Generalities

The name "sunstone" originates from the very nature of its properties known to communicate joy and to transmit light.

Lithotherapy

· Has a close affinity with the solar plexus

· Dispels stress, anxiety, and fear

· Facilitates positive self-affirmations and teaches how to say no

· Encourages healthy detachment and facilitates the removal of "hooks" remaining in the aura from past or present codependent relationships

· Communicates the art and joy of living

· Fights depression and seasonal mood disorders

· Helps to free oneself from feelings of inferiority

· Transmits a sense of self-worth and self-confidence

· Promotes optimism and the will to act

· Reveals new perspectives to the most inveterate pessimists

· Stimulates the neurovegetative system as well as auto-immune defenses

· Ensures harmonious cooperation between the organs

· Eases chronic sore throats

· Relieves gastric ulcers

· Facilitates weight loss

· Helps with sexual problems and disorders of the reproductive organs

· Purifies the kidneys, bladder, and intestines

· Eases problems of the spinal column

· Relieves rheumatism, arthritis, and general difficulties related to cartilage

This stone is especially effective when used outside in the sun.

TEKTITE

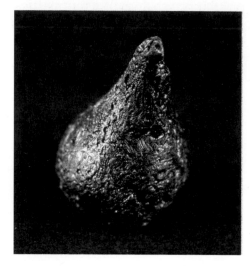

Crystal System: amorphous

Colors: black, brown black

Chakra: root

Hardness: 5 to 5.5

Origin: Czech Republic, Tibet

Formation Process: metamorphic

Chemical Composition: silicon oxide

Purification: occasionally cold water, incense, sunlight, earth

Recharging: quartz cluster, sunlight

Generalities

As with most black stones, Tibetan tektite is known to provide reliable protection from unwanted energies. It is considered a cousin of obsidian, and it works harmoniously with lapis lazuli, all types of quartz, jasper, chalcedony, and opal. Petrified wood has been known to contribute to grounding the strong energies of tektite without overpowering its positive effects.

Lithotherapy

· Possesses a particularly elevated vibration

· Increases the quality of the vibration of the auric field when it is worn

· Helps the body integrate high-frequency energies (right to the cellular level) that have proven vital for the evolution of humanity

· Holds the power to increase communication with other dimensions

· Encourages the feeling of being home here on earth for those who feel they originate from elsewhere and have a difficult time integrating here

- Elevates the consciousness beyond the vibration of the physical plane

- Facilitates the emotional release of undesirable events and assists in the assimilation of the lessons learned, by focusing one's mind on what contributes to spiritual growth

- Guides one to the heart of a problem or a difficulty so as to understand its true cause and undertake the necessary actions to remedy it

- Expels energetic residues, hence freeing the energy body and making it more receptive

- Stabilizes the flow of energy when placed on the chakras

- Balances the masculine and feminine energies

- Purifies the lower chakras, allowing one to remain grounded all the while maintaining a greater awareness

- Reduces fever

- Strengthens the capillaries and improves circulation

- Helps to prevent the transmission of infectious disease

TIGER EYE

Crystal System: trigonal

Colors: shimmering nuances of golden yellow and brown

Chakras: hara, solar plexus, root

Hardness: 7

Origin: Australia, Brazil, United States

Formation Process: sedimentary

Chemical Composition: silicon oxide

Purification: cold water, salt water, incense, sunlight, earth

Recharging: quartz cluster, sunlight

Generalities

In the Middle Ages, tiger eye was worn in the form of an amulet in order to ward off evil spells, demons, and the "evil eye."

Lithotherapy

- Resonates with the energy of the solar plexus
- Unites the energies of heaven and earth (anchors and elevates)
- Dissipates fear and anxiety
- Balances mood swings and stabilizes the emotions
- Aids hypochondriacs and eases psychosomatic ailments
- Confers strength, will, courage, and self-confidence
- Supports one during challenging times
- Protects and guards against harmful influences and unwanted energies
- Stabilizes confusing and complicated situations
- Confers the power to make decisions with a clear mind unclouded by emotions
- Improves the capacity to objectively perceive a problem or difficulty
- Treats ailments of the neck, throat, and eyes
- Benefits the reproductive organs
- Strengthens the spine by releasing toxins and easing pain
- Assists with the treatment of broken bones
- Soothes hyperstimulated nerves
- Calms an overactivity of the adrenal glands

In order to fully benefit from the virtues of tiger eye, it is recommended to wear it or place it directly on the skin. To anchor spiritual energies, it is suggested to place it in the navel area for a limited period of time. To benefit from its protective force, it can be worn for extended periods as a ring, earrings, or necklace, with occasional contact for short intervals on the solar plexus.

TIGER IRON (TIGERITE)

Crystal System: trigonal

Colors: layered aggregates of red jasper, black and metallic gray iron oxides (magnetite, hematite) and golden brown tiger eye

Chakras: hara, solar plexus, root

Hardness: 7

Origin: Australia, Brazil, India, South Africa, United States

Formation Process: metamorphic

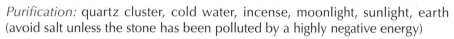

Chemical Composition: iron and silicon oxide

Purification: quartz cluster, cold water, incense, moonlight, sunlight, earth (avoid salt unless the stone has been polluted by a highly negative energy)

Recharging: quartz cluster, moonlight

Generalities

Tiger iron possesses the qualities of red jasper, hematite, and tiger eye. The properties of iron are concentrated and channeled by the tiger eye.

Lithotherapy

· Embodies force, audacity, and energy

· Revitalizes apathetic and despondent people

· Rejuvenates and invigorates in cases of great fatigue

· Recharges the solar plexus

· Eases traumas that cause depression

· Encourages facing one's fears

· Stimulates the mind and intellectual acuity

· Develops a sense of constructive self-criticism

- Helps to re-instate equilibrium following shock or trauma

- Reinforces and purifies the bloodstream, thereby acting as a prevention to illnesses of the blood

- Stimulates the blood flow

- Diminishes sensations of heaviness in the legs

- Regulates the heart rate

- Recommended for athletes who must make arduous and sustained efforts

- Reinforces the muscular structure

- Contributes to healthy scarring of the tissues

- Stimulates the taste buds

TOPAZ FAMILY

Crystal System: rhombic

Colors: green blue, clear brown, golden yellow, reddish pink, green

Chakras: heart, crown, throat, third eye

Hardness: 8

Origin: Australia, Brazil, Japan, Madagascar, Myanmar, Mexico, Nigeria, Russia, Sri Lanka, United States

Formation Process: magmatic

Chemical Composition: aluminum silicate with fluorine

Purification: cold water, salt water, incense, sunlight, earth

Recharging: quartz cluster, abundance of sunlight

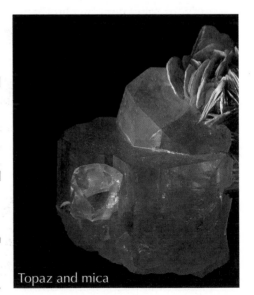

Topaz and mica

Generalities

Topaz is considered to be the stone of Jupiter, a planet thought to greatly influence the direction of one's life. Ancient civilizations therefore recognized its ability to grant one the power to control one's life. Golden topaz is associated with the sun, while blue topaz spreads this solar fire throughout the sky.

Lithotherapy

· Accentuates innate capacities and brings forth latent talents
· Predisposes one to truth, candor, and honesty
· Confers joy, abundance, and health
· Purifies the aura
· Neutralizes negative energies within the personality as well as in the environment
· Induces relaxation by eliminating tension
· Inspires self-confidence
· Facilitates the expression of ideas
· Encourages a philanthropic attitude
· Sharpens and reinforces the intellect
· Aligns and recharges the meridians
· Facilitates digestion
· Fights anorexia
· Activates the metabolism
· Promotes the process of recovery and regeneration following surgery
· Improves blood circulation, thereby warming cold extremities
· Treats varicose veins as well as cardiovascular problems
· Fights exhaustion and insomnia
· Revitalizes the liver
· Stimulates the taste buds
· Fortifies the nerves

BLUE TOPAZ

Lithotherapy

- Connected to the angelic realm, particularly the angels of truth and wisdom

- Enhances meditation

- Contributes to living life according to one's true aspirations

- Improves verbal expression

- Eases ailments of the throat

- Stimulates the renal functions

- Treats head injuries and general afflictions of the head and skull

- Alleviates occipital pains, jaw clenching, and migraines

- Improves verbal expression

CLEAR TOPAZ

Lithotherapy

- Reveals the karmic consequences of one's actions

- Purifies negative emotions

- Facilitates insight and realizations

- Dissipates stagnant energies

GOLD TOPAZ (IMPERIAL TOPAZ)

Lithotherapy

· Revitalizes the body and mind

· Augments faith and optimism

· Encourages harmony with the higher forces

· Facilitates access to akashic archives

· Contributes to the recognition of one's own faculties

· Improves confidence

· Inspires one to overcome limitations

· Regenerates cellular structures

· Facilitates recovery from nervous exhaustion and burn out

· Aids with the assimilation of nutrients

· Treats the liver and gallbladder

· Balances the endocrine glands

PINK TOPAZ

Lithotherapy

· Reinstates faith

· Gently eliminates uneasiness

· Offers the possibility to perceive the face of the Divine

TOURMALINE FAMILY

Crystal System: trigonal

Colors: blue, yellow, black, pink green

Chakras: according to color

Hardness: 7 to 7.5

Origin: Australia, Brazil, India, Italy, Madagascar, Myanmar, Russia, United States

Formation Process: magmatic

Chemical Composition: complex boron, sodium, aluminum, iron, magnesium and calcium silicate

Purification: cold water, salt water, incense, sunlight, earth

Recharging: quartz cluster, sunlight

Generalities

Tourmaline will transmit its beneficial effects to various parts of the body according to its particular color. Its natural ridges act as conductors of high-frequency energy, which make it an ideal stone for treating, whether it is used to direct a particular energy to an area in need or to gradually dissipate certain blockages. Multicolored tourmaline is a superb transmitter that unites the properties of each of the respective colors.

Lithotherapy

· Considered to be a symbol of clear wisdom, it unveils all forms of injustice and wrong action

· Helps to build the bridge between the soul and the mental, astral, and physical bodies to create a harmonious, working unity

· Awakens creativity

· Supports imagination, visualization, and creative dreams

- Carries and increases the quantity of light and energy anywhere it is used

- Balances the chakras and the meridians

- Creates a protective shield around the bodies

- Cleanses, purifies, and transforms any dense energy into a lighter vibration

- Purifies the aura

- Removes blockages

- Eliminates the feeling of being a victim

- Invites inspiration, compassion, tolerance, and prosperity

- Transforms negative thoughts into positive ones

- Calms paranoia

- Stimulates the metabolism, hormonal glands, and the immune system

- Balances the cerebral hemispheres

- Supports those with dyslexia

Black Tourmaline (Schorl)

Lithotherapy

- Anchors and grounds, being especially useful following a treatment by helping those who have not fully integrated into their body

- Protects from negative energies

- When used with mica, it reflects the negative energies back to the person to be worked out by the person responsible

- Neutralizes the effects of radiation
- Deflects harmful vibrations coming from electrical equipment (cellular phones, computers, televisions, etc.)
- Relieves pain and redirects unbalanced bodily energies
- Confers neutrality and serenity by activating a clear and logical reasoning
- Alleviates stress and tension caused by an excessive workload
- Stabilizes mental deviations and digressions, thereby helping to prevent insanity
- Regenerates the female reproductive system, thereby aiding menstrual problems such as cramps, and ovarian cysts
- Alleviates problems caused by scarring

BLUE TOURMALINE (INDICOLITE)

Lithotherapy

- Activates the throat and third eye chakras
- Treats throat, lung, and eye problems
- Enhances communication and intuition necessary for contact with other worlds
- Appeases and dissipates sadness and suppressed emotions
- Intensifies the aspiration toward freedom of mind
- Calms mental agitation and incessant thoughts
- Aligns the mental processes
- Increases tolerance and the sense of responsibility
- Ensures the equilibrium of the organic fluids
- Regenerates the kidneys and bladder

- Soothes burns and prevents scars

- Eases skin problems of a psychosomatic nature

- Alleviates sinusitis

- Supports the brain and balances the brain hemispheres

- Treats the heart and lungs

- Stimulates the thymus and strengthens the immune system

- Benefits the throat and thyroid (which may encourage weight loss)

- Treats bacterial infections

GREEN TOURMALINE (VERDELITE)

Lithotherapy

- Known as the "Stone of Universal Healing," thereby benefiting the body and the mind

- Encourages love and compassion as it possesses an affinity with the heart chakra

- Reveals emotional issues and facilitates their release

- Confers patience and openness, permitting one to perceive many solutions in any given situation

- Liberates one from past-life traumas

- Dissolves stress and fears, thereby conferring tranquillity

- Promotes peaceful sleep

- Conveys a *joie de vivre* and renders one grateful for the miracles of life

- Strengthens the nervous system, hence providing a greater resistance to stress and fatigue

- Develops the sense of touch and smell, and restores the taste buds

- Tones the heart

- Detoxifies the body, favoring elimination

- Relieves constipation and diarrhea

- Benefits hyperactive children.

PINK TOURMALINE (RUBELLITE)

Lithotherapy

- Encourages correct goal orientation and proper evaluation of motives, based on heart wisdom and clarity of mind

- Intimately tuned to the heart chakra, it communicates joy and unconditional love

- Generates profound relaxation

- Communicates peace and security

- Supports those who have been abused

- Encourages freedom from past emotional wounds, while communicating trust and the courage to love

- Comforts during periods of grief

- Stimulates the desire to face life and relationships with enthusiasm and joy, without fears or barriers

- Benefits the heart and lungs

- Eases skin problems

- Improves the flow of energy in the physical and subtle bodies and ameliorates nerve conduction

Watermelon Tourmaline

Lithotherapy

· Activates the heart chakra through its gentle potency

· Transmits its energies lightly and harmoniously, thus being particularly favorable for children

· Grants love, tenderness, and friendship

· Instills patience

· Encourages tact and diplomacy

· Generally beneficial for relationships

· Facilitates the comprehension of situations and the expression of one's intentions

· Relieves stress and promotes inner security

· Encourages finding joy in every situation

· Facilitates liberation from old emotional wounds

· Alleviates depression and soothes fears

· Activates nerve regeneration, especially in cases of paralysis or multiple sclerosis

Yellow Tourmaline (Dravite)

Lithotherapy

· Regenerates the solar plexus

· Stimulates simple and imaginative creativity

· Sharpens the intellect

· Confers mental clarity

· Instills a sense of courage and personal power

*

· Supports those involved in business endeavours

· Benefits the stomach, spleen, gallbladder, and kidneys

· Activates a sense of community, service, and social commitment

· Sharpens and strengthens manual skills

· Revives the regenerative power of cells, tissues, and organs

Turquoise

Crystal System: triclinic

Colors: blue, turquoise, green

Chakras: all, although mainly the heart, throat, hara, solar plexus and third eye

Hardness: 5 to 6

Origin: Afghanistan, Austria, China, Iran, Israel, Tanzania

Formation Process: sedimentary

Chemical Composition: basic hydrated aluminum and copper phosphate

Purification: cold water, incense, earth

Recharging: quartz cluster, limited sunlight

Generalities

To this day, turquoise is known to possess a protective power against malicious forces. It is recognized as an ancient stone of power.

Lithotherapy

· Aligns, balances, and fortifies all the chakras and meridians

· Purifies the throat chakra, thereby activating effective oral and written communication, and allowing for the expression of true emotion

· Balances mood swings

· Assists in recovery following depression

· Calms the nervous system

· Prevents panic attacks

· Transmits the message that one is responsible for one's own happiness

· Clarifies the faulty view of being a victim of life and eliminates the martyr complex

· Revitalizes by providing strength and drive when one is exhausted or discouraged

· Provides for a consistent inner tranquility while awakening vivacity and the desire to take action

· Protects from unhealthy external influences or atmospheric pollutants

· Awakens the intuition

· Possesses a strong capacity to regenerate and protect, providing overall health and strength

· Balances the cholesterol level

· Detoxifies, thereby acting as an analgesic, antispasmodic, and anti-inflammatory agent

· Neutralizes hyperacidity

· Relieves symptoms of gout and rheumatism

· Helps fight viral infections

- Soothes sore throats
- Eases respiratory conditions
- Soothes stomach problems
- Increases muscular strength
- Fortifies the blood and stimulates circulation
- Generates inner heat in order to warm the body
- Regenerates tissues
- Stimulates cerebral activity as well as sensory perception

Turquoise is often worn as an amulet for protection, and it has been known to change color as a warning of impending danger. Placed on the third eye, it increases intuition and intensifies meditation.

VARISCITE (UTAHITE)

*

Crystal System: rhombic

Colors: colorless, green, gray, and white

Chakras: heart, solar plexus

Hardness: 4-5

Origin: Austria, Australia, Bolivia, Czech Republic, Germany, Unites States

Formation Process: sedimentary

Chemical Composition: hydrated aluminium phosphate

Purification: distilled water, avoid salt

Recharging: quartz cluster, sunlight

Generalities

Variscite, also known as utahite, is a stone that closely resembles turquoise. It is a stone of authenticity and truthfulness that contributes to acknowledging one's faults in order to change them. Variscite will support those who have lost faith and who need to reconcile with the Divine or God.

Lithotherapy

- Lifts the spirits
- Confers courage and re-instills a sense of self-confidence hence eliminating feelings of inferiority
- Encourages one to remain hopeful even in the most difficult situations
- Supports those suffering from illnesses or chronic health difficulties
- Teaches caregivers how to deal with an illness by bringing unconditional love into the situation
- Facilitates past-life exploration
- Attracts abundance
- Stabilizes the emotional and physical body
- Instills unconditional love and harmony
- Enhances maternal tenderness
- Reinforces friendship and understanding by eradicating negative influences
- Enhances learning abilities and a clear thinking process
- Contributes to self-expression and the communication of ideas
- Calms the nervous system and invites peace and harmony to environments, people, and situations
- Restores depleted energy reserves, thereby helping in cases of chronic fatigue
- Neutralizes stress-related difficulties
- Is beneficial for gout, hyperacidity, stomach ulcers, and rheumatism
- Supports the blood and heart
- Strengthens the heart muscles
- Improves vision
- Benefits the lungs and back

VESUVIANITE (IDOCRASE)

Crystal System: quadratic

Colors: ochre olive green to orange brown

Chakras: hara, solar plexus, heart

Hardness: 6.5 to 7

Origin: Canada, Italy, Russia, United States

Formation Process: metamorphic

Chemical Composition: complex basic calcaro-magnesic, aluminum and iron silicate

Purification: cold water, salt water, incense, sunlight, earth

Recharging: quartz cluster, abundance of sunlight

Generalities

Vesuvianite is a stone that offers support in the personal battle between the ego and the Self. It serves as a guide on the path to achieving one's true life purpose.

Lithotherapy

· Liberates one from feelings of confinement

· Contributes to healing past lives and to liberating oneself from mental and emotional prisons

· Gently dissipates anger and neutralizes negative thought patterns

· Alleviates symptoms of depression

· Acts as a support to combat fear

· Broadens the mind

· Stimulates creativity and the need for discovery

· Facilitates the assimilation of nutrients

· Restores the sense of smell

· Fortifies tooth enamel

· Benefits the kidneys and bladder

WULFENITE

Crystal System: quadratic

Colors: from honey yellow to orange yellow, vermilion red

Chakras: hara, solar plexus

Hardness: 3

Origin: Austria, Democratic Republic of the Congo, Mexico, Morocco, Namibia, Slovenia, United States, Yugoslavia

Formation Process: sedimentary

Chemical Composition: lead molybdenum oxide

Purification: cold water, incense, sunlight

Recharging: quartz cluster, abundance of sunlight

Generalities

Wulfenite's properties are similar to those of amber in that it possesses the power to gently activate the chakra on which it is placed. It can also be programmed to initiate contact with one's soul group.

Lithotherapy

· Prevents discouragement

· Benefits those in a state of imbalance

· Supports the recognition and integration of the shadow side of the self

- Acts as a mirror for those who have become superficial or false, thereby allowing for correction of these very aspects
- Favors rejuvenation and fights aging
- Preserves energy
- Activates the renal functions and treats the pancreas
- Alleviates chronic throat problems

ZINCITE

Crystal System: hexagonal

Colors: red, reddish brown, orange yellow, green, translucent

Chakras: hara, root, solar plexus

Hardness: 4

Origin: Italy, Poland, United States

Formation Process: unknown

Chemical Composition: zinc oxide

Purification: distilled salt water, cold water, incense, moonlight, sunlight

Recharging: quartz cluster, moonlight, sunlight

Generalities

Zincite was accidentally discovered in the pipes of industrial ovens destined to produce zinc in Poland. This gem is consequently considered both synthetic and natural, having not been intentionally fabricated by humans. Zincite from Poland is becoming more and more rare, yet it is still highly sought after on the international market.

Lithotherapy

- Anchors spiritual aspirations to the physical plane
- Increases energy and vitality
- Instills courage, passion, and will power
- Ignites the fires of creativity
- Recharges a depleted solar plexus with energy, thus inviting determination, perseverance and the ability to manifest intentions
- Confers the final impulse necessary for the completion of long term projects
- Amplifies the energy of the majority of other stones
- Facilitates the acceptance of change when necessary
- Contributes to finding the cause of a phobia and to freeing oneself from it
- Promotes group work and cooperative activity, drawing like-minded people together
- Arouses sexual desire
- Supports the prostate
- Increases fertility, revives the reproductive organs, and alleviates menstrual symptoms
- Stimulates the meridians and all the systems within the body
- Stimulates the endocrine and immune systems
- Benefits the skin and hair
- Activates the organs related to assimilation and elimination

ZIRCON

Crystal System: quadratic

Colors: blue, brown, clear, orange yellow, red.

Chakras: according to color

Hardness: 7.5

Origin: Australia, Brazil, Cambodia, France, Madagascar, Myanmar, Tanzania, Thailand, Vietnam

Formation Process: magmatic

Chemical Composition: zirconium silicate

Purification: cold water, salt water, incense, sunlight, earth

Recharging: quartz cluster, sunlight

Generalities

Zircon is not recommended for those prone to stress or anger. The presence of hafnium, thorium, and uranium (up to 10 percent) may render this stone radioactive. In antiquity, it was believed that zircon could heal madness.

Lithotherapy

· Encourages reflection on the meaning of existence

· Contributes to overcoming feelings of grief

· Helps one to become conscious of the transitory nature of things

· Invites reflection on what is truly important in life

· Stimulates the liver

· Eases pain

· Treats menstrual symptoms and alleviates cramps

ZOISITE

Crystal System: rhombic

Colors: green, brownish green with red (ruby)

Chakras: heart, root, third eye

Hardness: 6.5 to 7

Origin: Australia, Cambodia, India, Kenya, Madagascar, Russia, South Africa, Sri Lanka, Tanzania

Formation Process: metamorphic

Chemical Composition: basic aluminium and limestone silicate with manganese

Purification: cold water, incense, sunlight, earth

Recharging: quartz cluster, sunlight

Generalities

In moments of indecisiveness, zoisite inspires the capacity to make enlightened and authentic choices. It is recommended to work with zoisite on a consistent basis, as it is known to take time before demonstrating its effect.

Lithotherapy

- Transforms negative energies into positive one's
- Encourages breaking free from the influence of others
- Allows one to reconnect with true desires and intentions, thereby allowing for the attainment of authentic dreams and goals
- Enhances creativity
- Transforms destructive attitudes into a more constructive lifestyle
- Eliminates lethargy

- Uncovers suppressed emotions to allow for their expression
- Encourages rest and recovery following an illness or difficult circumstances
- Increases fertility and stimulates the sexual energy
- Treats testicular and ovarian conditions
- Strengthens the immune system
- Detoxifies and neutralizes hyperacidity and inflammation

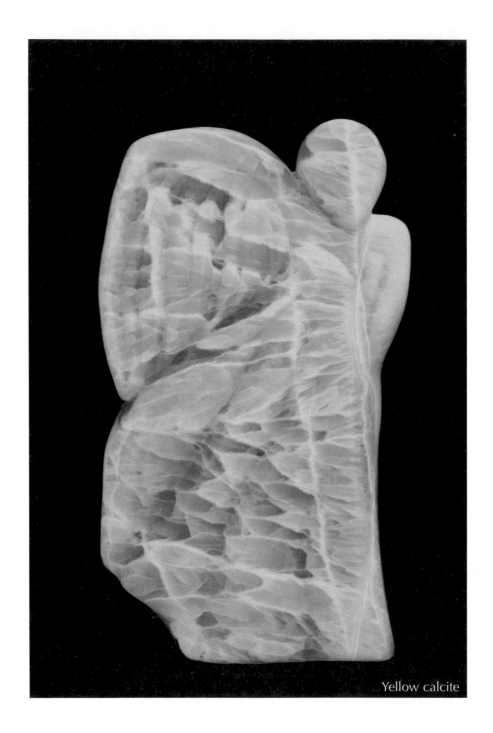

Yellow calcite

250

INDEX OF AILMENTS AND STONES

In this section, we have included the most common physical and emotional ailments, accompanied by stones that can bring relief. We would like to point out that any health improvement is the result of the chemical and energetic symbiosis between the mineral kingdom and the human kingdom, and not from the user himself or herself.

Acidity

andalusite-chiastolite: alleviates hyperacidity

bloodstone (heliotrope): neutralizes excesses of acidity

malachite: diminishes acidity, in the tissues

turquoise: diminishes excessive acidity, neutralizes hyperacidity

uvarovite garnet: treats acidosis (high level of acidity in the blood)

variscite: neutralizes excessive acidity

zoisite: detoxifies, neutralizes excessive acidity and inflammation

Allergies

amber: diminishes allergic reactions

apophyllite: neutralizes allergies

aquamarine: alleviates allergic reactions

aventurine: calms allergies

danburite: alleviates allergies

fluorite: eases the psychological cause of allergies

golden obsidian: fights allergies

lepidolite: relieves allergy symptoms

rhodochrosite: alleviates skin allergies

Anemia

coral: alleviates anemia following disease or in the presence of low immunity

hematite: relieves blood disorders such as anemia

magnetite: alleviates anemia

pyrope garnet: alleviates anemia

violet spinel: balances low blood pressure, anemia, and other blood diseases

Anger

blue lace agate: neutralizes anger

amazonite: dissolves anger

amethyst: calms anger

andalousite/chiastolite (green): releases emotional blockages, particularly those caused by accumulated anger

apatite: helps to overcome sorrow, anger, and inertia

aragonite: supports one during periods of stress and anger

green calcite: calms discomfort generated by anger

chrysoprase: decreases anger

citrine: eliminates anger

red garnet: helps to control anger, especially the anger which is directed toward oneself

howlite: helps to calm uncontrolled anger

kyanite: dissipates anger

peridot: helps the healing of a wounded ego by attenuating anger

rose quartz: activates forgiveness and decreases anger and resentment

rhodonite: dissolves resentment, anger

ruby: allows anger and negativity to surface in order to be eliminated

blue topaz: helps to control anger

vesuvianite: gently dissipates anger

Anorexia

fluorite: fights anorexia

spessartite garnet: excels in treating anorexia, is considered the stone that stimulates the appetite

lepidolite: helps to overcome any type of emotional dependency and treats anorexia

topaz: stimulates the appetite and helps in cases of anorexia

Antibiotic

amber: acts as an antibiotic

Anxiety

aquamarine: calms anxiety

azurite-malachite: diminishes anxiety, encourages the transcendence of fears

lepidolite: calms anxiety caused by annoyances and stressful events

malachite: releases anxiety

sapphire: soothes anxiety

sodalite: acts against anxiety, inviting confidence and humility

Arthritis

blue lace agate: diminishes inflammation as well as the deformations caused by arthritis

apatite: soothes arthritis

azurite-malachite: alleviates joint problems (arthritis)

green calcite: alleviates arthritis

carnelian: relieves the problems of arthritis

fluorite: restores mobility to the joints and alleviates arthritis

garnet: brings relief to those who suffer from rheumatism and arthritis (direct application or in the form of an elixir)

hematite: excels against pain in the joints and bones (such as arthritis, leg cramps, fractures)

jet: absorbs inflammation such as that caused by arthritis

malachite: diminishes the pain caused by arthritis

obsidian: alleviates the pain caused by arthritis, soothes pain in the joints as well as in the muscles

rhodonite: treats inflammation of the joints due to arthritis

turquoise: fights rheumatism and arthritis

Asthma

apophyllite: soothes asthma attacks

azurite-malachite: helps diminishes asthma

pink beryl (morganite): oxygenates and reorganizes the cells, which proves to be beneficial in countering asthma

cat's eye (cymophane): excels in countering asthma

gem silica: helps in the cases of bronchitis or asthma

malachite: helps to diminish asthma

pyrite: is beneficial for the lungs, relieves asthma and bronchitis

rhodochrosite: relieves asthma; absorbs irritants, thereby soothing respiratory difficulties

Bacteria

amber: acts as an antibiotic

green calcite: helps the body to eliminate bacterial infections

iolite (water sapphire): helps destroy bacteria

lazurite: eliminates bacteria

sulfur: is regarded as a powerful purifier, antibacterial, and antiparasitic

blue tourmaline(indicolite): eliminates bacterial infections

Bladder

agate: reduces inflammation of the bladder

carnelian: strengthens the bladder

citrine: treats bladder infections

diamond: strengthens the bladder

grossular garnet: helps to regulates the urinary system

magnetite jade: treats the kidneys and the bladder

jasper: is beneficial for the bladder

prehnite : regulates the renal glands and strengthens the bladder

serpentine : supports the bladder

sunstone: purifies the bladder and treats infections

blue tourmaline (indicolite): activates the kidneys and the bladder

vesuvianite: facilitates the proper functioning of the kidneys and bladder

Blood

amethyst: purifies the blood

ametrine: purifies the blood

bloodstone (heliotrope): purifies the blood, controls and supports blood circulation as well as organs rich in blood

calcite: stimulates the coagulation of blood and treats the tissues and bones

carnelian: treats blood poisoning

chalcedony: improves the quality of blood and its circulation

blue chalcedony: ensures a good circulation of the organic fluids (lymph, blood, etc.)

citrine: detoxifies the blood and increases blood circulation

coral: improves blood circulation and increases the blood's iron content

black coral: purifies the blood

red coral: supports the coagulation of blood in wounds

cordierite (water sapphire): treats blood diseases

fluorite: activates blood circulation

andradite garnet: helps with the production of hemoglobin

pyrope garnet: improves circulation and the quality of blood, controls disorders of the heart, blood pressure, and blood circulation

rhodolite garnet: treats blood poisoning

uvarovite garnet: treats acidosis (high acidity of the blood), helps in cases of leukemia, and helps the liver to purify blood

blue halite: supports the lymphatic system and the blood

hematite: supports the formation of hemoglobin and stops hemorrhages, particularly effective in cases of anemia, increases the quality of blood and reduces blood pressure

kunzite: supports healthy blood circulation

obsidian: improves blood circulation, even in extreme cases

fire opal: strengthens blood circulation

petrified wood: purifies the liver and blood

pyrite: oxygenates the blood and strengthens the circulatory system

rhodochrosite: improves elasticity of the blood vessels, thereby diminishing tension and relieving migraines; purifies the blood; strengthens the heart, and reduces heart palpitations

ruby: detoxifies the blood

sapphire: helps with diseases of the blood

tiger iron: re-energizes and purifies the blood, making it effective against blood diseases; improves circulation

topaz: increases blood circulation, thereby warming and supporting the limbs

turquoise: activates blood circulation and regenerates tissues

Blood Pressure

aventurine: balances the blood pressure and stimulates the metabolism

blue calcite: regulates blood pressure

charoite: regulates blood pressure

almandine garnet: regulates blood pressure, improves blood circulation

hematite: increases the quality of the blood and reduces blood pressure

kyanite: decreases blood pressure

malachite: lowers blood pressure

piertersite: stimulates the pituitary gland, thereby balancing the endocrine system and the production of hormones, which governs the metabolism and blood pressure

rhodocrosite: normalizes blood pressure

sodalite: lowers blood pressure

Body Odors

orbicular jasper: eliminates toxins that generate body odors

magnesite: detoxifies and neutralizes body odors

Brain (Imbalance)

blue lace agate: taken in the form of an elixir, it acts on imbalances of the cerebral fluids and hydrocephalus

amazonite: strengthens the nerves and alleviates certain diseases of the brain

amber: balances the hemispheres of the brain

amethyst: facilitates the operation of the right hemisphere of the brain

carnelian: activates the brain cells

citrine: stimulates the brain cells

danburite: balances the hemispheres of the brain

epidote: relieves disorders of the brain

fluorite: facilitates the activity of the nervous system, in particular the brain cells

kyanite: acts effectively on the brain

lepidolite: improves neural connections in the brain

moonstone: awakens the intuitive side of the brain

pyrite: stimulates mental activity by increasing blood circulation to the brain

sapphire: acts on disorders of the nervous system (brain and nerves)

selenite: stimulates the brain, memory, and the intellect

sodalite: soothes the nerves and brain

blue tourmaline: balances the hemispheres, aligns the mental processes

Bronchitis

cat's eye (cymophane): benefits the bronchial tubes

gem silica: helps in cases of bronchitis

hawk eye: purifies the bronchial tubes

pyrite: is beneficial for the lungs, alleviating asthma and bronchitis

pyrolusite: eases cases of bronchitis and regularizes metabolism

rutilated quartz: benefits symptoms of bronchitis and asthma, effective for general respiratory disorders and chronic bronchitis

Cancer

azeztulite: supports cancer treatments

coral: supports bone cancer treatments

melanite garnet: collaborates in treatments against cancer

petalite: supports the treatment of cancer and AIDS

Cardiovascular

kunzite: reinforces the cardiovascular system

rose quartz: reinforces the heart

Cartilage

amber: eases joint problems and supports the formation of cartilage

apatite: facilitates the regeneration of the cells as well as the formation of cartilage

larimar: acts effectively on the cartilage

sunstone: relieves problems of the cartilage

Cellulitis (Cellulite)

yellow apatite: reduces cellulite

citrine: diminishes cellulite

Chemotherapy

prophesy stone: supports the body through chemotherapy and radiotherapy treatments

smoky quartz: helps during radiation and chemotherapy treatments

Cholesterol

aventurine: balances the blood pressure, stimulates the metabolism and decreases cholesterol

yellow fluorite: reduces cholesterol

magnesite: accelerates fat metabolism, dissolves cholesterol (accelerates decomposition)

turquoise: reduces cholesterol

Clarity of Mind

agate: balances and harmonizes body, mind, and spirit

blue lace agate: instills peace and tranquility and leads to high states of awareness

amber: purifies the emotional, mental, and physical body

amethyst: calms or stimulates the mind according to need

ametrine: releases blockages in the emotional and mental bodies

angel aura quartz: contributes to the elimination of restrictive beliefs and erroneous mental attitudes

apatite: balances the mind

azurite: clarifies the mind and allows for the understanding of the psychosomatic effects of the mind and emotions on the body

yellow calcite: encourages mental flexibility by exposing the concrete mind to higher mental energies; its energy is highly expansive

chrysoprase: develops clarity of mind

coral: favors good mental health

danburite: elevates the vibrations of the mental body, which thereby stimulates purification

emerald: helps to maintain mental equilibrium

green fluorite: purifies the mental body

jasper (veined with hematite): eliminates excessive energy accumulated in the head and supports mental clarity

lepidolite: helps to overcome any type of emotional or mental dependency

obsidian: breaks mental barriers and conditioning

snowflake obsidian: balances the body, mind, and spirit

white opal: brings clarity of mind and spontaneity

peridot: purifies the subtle bodies, including the mind

piertesite: eliminates mental conditioning

pyrite: stimulates the memory and intellectual faculties (organization, management, order, structure, planning, etc.)

sapphire: produces peace of mind

tiger eye: brings clarity to confusion, thereby encouraging objectivity and constructive decision making

blue topaz: releases the mind from limited rationalization and narrow convictions

yellow tourmaline: confers clarity of mind

Communication

amazonite: encourages communication

apatite: supports communication

aqua aura quartz: encourages sincere communication

aquamarine: favors communication

aragonite: stimulates communication on higher levels

blue calcite: facilitates clear communication

celestite: supports clear ideas and fluid communication

chalcedony: supports one during telepathic communication or transmission

blue chalcedony: helps to develop active listening and constructive communication

chrysocolla: improves communication by supporting discernment

blue fluorite: intensifies creative thinking, logical thought, and communication

gem silica: facilitates clarity in communication as well as telepathic rapport

howlite: encourages calm and reasonable communication

kunzite: supports loving and respectful communication

kyanite: facilitates creative expression and communication

lapis lazuli: stimulates communication

pietersite: facilitates eloquent speech

sapphire: helps to develop communication skills

sodalite: supports the verbal expression of feelings

sugilite: encourages loving communication

tibetan tektite: helps to communicate with other worlds

blue tourmaline (indicolite): encourages communication skills and stimulates the intuition, which can open the door to other worlds and dimensions

turquoise: activates oral and written communication and the expression of true feelings

Concentration

natural agate: facilitates concentration

amber: facilitates concentration

ametrine: eliminates stress and tension in the head, allowing for better concentration in meditation and clarity of thought

yellow apatite: activates concentration

aqua aura quartz: activates the third eye, bringing concentration and clear thinking

carnelian: facilitates concentration

fluorite: vitalizes the mind and stimulates concentration

lapis lazuli: stimulates concentration and presence of mind

moonstone and cat's eye (cymophane): helps with concentration during meditation or when experiencing mental fatigue

onyx: helps with concentration and in the event of memory loss

sapphire: stimulates concentration

selenite: increases concentration and clear thinking

tibetan tektite: facilitates the release of undesirable events and assimilation of lessons learned by allowing one to contemplate on what contributes to spiritual growth

Constipation

calcite (orange, red): helps to eliminate all that is stagnant, including the cause of constipation

citrine: relieves constipation

grossular garnet: relieves constipation

reddish-brown jasper: alleviates constipation and other digestion problems, stimulates the proper functioning of the liver

green tourmaline (verdelite): detoxifies and treats constipation

Dependencies

fire agate: treats addictions

white agate: helps to overcome dependencies when used with ruby

amethyst: helps fight addiction to drugs, alcohol, and tobacco, among others

aventurine: benefits those with a gambling addiction

iolite: leads to the comprehension and release of certain addictive habits

kunzite: helps to release one from emotional dependency

lepidolite: helps to overcome any type of emotional or mental dependency

Depression

Botswana agate: eases depression

amber: fights depression

ametrine: helps in the event of depression

yellow apatite: extracts stagnant energy and treats apathy and depression

black calcite: helps fight depression and encourages one to face and combat the darker aspects of the personality

orange calcite: helps to overcome depression

carnelian: helps to banish negative emotions that feed depressive states

chalcedony: is beneficial in the event of depression

citrine: eases depression and provides release from oppressive influences

coral: replenishes depleted energy and helps to overcome depression

epidote: contributes to overcoming self-destructive emotions that can cause depression

garnet: fights nervous breakdown and burnout

gem silica: releases from feelings of depression and self-deprecation

hematite: brings strength and energy during depression

kunzite: contains lithium and is thereby beneficial to counter depression and certain psychiatric ailments

white opal: alleviates worries, chronic stress, and depression

piertersite (chestnut color): helps to neutralize suicidal thoughts and treats depression

pyrite: fights melancholy, depression, and intense despair

rose quartz: eases depression

rhodochrosite: acts against depression

sunstone: fights depression

tiger iron: eases traumas that lead to depression

watermelon tourmaline: alleviates depression and fear

turquoise: regenerates and rejuvenates in the event of depression

vesuvianite: banishes negative emotions that cause depression

Diabetes and Hypoglycemia

moss agate: helps to prevent hypoglycemia

calcite: benefits the pancreas and the spleen

carnelian: contributes to the healthy functioning of the digestive system, including the pancreas

cat's eye (cymophane): regulates the pancreas

blue chalcedony: regularizes the production of insulin and is thereby useful during the initial stages of diabetes

charoite: benefits the pancreas

chrysocolla: helps to balance the pancreas

citrine: treats diabetes

emerald: eases the symptoms of diabetes

almandine garnet: supports the liver and pancreas

malachite: eases the symptoms of diabetes when it is worn at the waist

moss opal: benefits the pancreas, spleen, and liver

serpentine: eases the symptoms of diabetes and hypoglycemia

Eczema

amber: helps to relieve allergies and eczema (ideal if worn as a necklace)

bismuth: relieves eczema and other skin diseases

lapis lazuli: relieves eczema

mook jasper (mokaïte): relieves eczema

dark blue sapphire: contributes to the treatment of skin diseases such as eczema

Emotional Exhaustion

apatite: overcomes emotional exhaustion

tiger iron: is useful for those who suffer from mental or emotional exhaustion

Emotions

amethyst: calms passions, violent emotions, and anger

andalusite-chiastolite: stabilizes the emotions and helps one to remain centered

apophyllite: releases repressed emotions

aquamarine: calms emotions

azurite: allows for the understanding of the psychosomatic effects of the mind and emotions on the body

azurite-malachite: helps to overcome pain and misfortune, to release and communicate repressed emotions, and to listen to one's feelings

boji stones: dissipates repressed emotions

orange calcite: balances the emotions

pink calcite: releases the physical tensions caused by blocked emotions and stress

red calcite: brings forth and releases pent-up passions and emotions

carnelian: helps to banish the negative emotions that cause depression such as fear

celestite: soothes fiery emotions

chalcedony: harmonizes emotions and dissipates negative feelings

chrysocolla: allows one to become aware of negative emotions

epidote: contributes to overcoming self-destructive emotions that can cause depression

fluorite: stabilizes the emotions

melanite garnet: opens one up to love when it has been lacking; dissipates anger, desire, jealousy, and mistrust

hawk eye: clarifies suppressed emotions and pain from former lives as well as the present life

howlite: calms the turbulent emotions that have their roots in former lives

kunzite: soothes the emotions and brings to the surface those which are repressed in order to face them

lapis lazuli: allows for the expression of feelings

larimar: eliminates excessive fears and calms emotions

lepidolite: is recognized to be one of the most powerful stones to soothe anxiety, fear, and grief and to neutralize destructive thoughts

malachite: absorbs negative emotions when placed at the solar plexus

moonstone: stabilizes the emotions, eases emotional instability and stress

blue opal: soothes the emotions related to the past and helps to express them

white opal: soothes the emotions and encourages a positive view

peridot: harmonizes and balances the emotions

rhodochrosite: invites spontaneity and helps one to express emotions

rhodonite: heals wounds of the past and self-destructive emotions

rutile: stabilizes the emotions

clear blue sapphire: soothes emotions

fishtail selenite: soothes and stabilizes the emotions and defuses tension

sodalite: helps to control the emotions and calms panic attacks

clear topaz: purifies negative emotions

pink tourmaline: moderates excessive emotions while allowing for the understanding of the cause

zoisite: brings to light repressed emotions so that they may be expressed

Endocrine System

amethyst: harmonizes the endocrine system and metabolism

yellow jasper: rejuvenates the endocrine system

pietersite: stimulates the pituitary gland, thereby balancing the endocrine system and the production of the hormones that govern metabolism

zincite: stimulates the endocrine system

Energy Blockages

apophyllite: releases blockages and helps to re-establish the proper circulation of energy in the meridians

boji stones: reveals and dissolves blockages

dioptase: reveals emotional blockages while stabilizing

melanite garnet: eliminates blockages in the heart and throat chakras

larimar: dissipates energy blockages in the chest, head, and neck

mahogany obsidian: anchors and protects, eliminates energy blockages that resonate with the earth

wulfenite: releases blockages

Gallbladder

yellow apatite: regulates the liver, pancreas, gallbladder, and spleen

azurite: regulates the gallbladder

orange calcite: regulates the gallbladder

carnelian: benefits the gallbladder

cat's eye (cymophane): regulates the gallbladder and liver chalcedony: contributes to the healthy functioning of the gallbladder

danburite: alleviates problems of the liver and gallbladder

epidote: stimulates the healthy functioning of the gallbladder

andradite garnet: helps with the dysfunction of the liver and the gallbladder

jasper: encourages healthy functioning of the bladder, gallbladder, and liver

golden obsidian: regulates the gallbladder

peridot: regenerates the gallbladder

petrified wood: regulates the liver and gallbladder

gold topaz: regulates the liver and gallbladder

yellow tourmaline: regulates the gallbladder

Headaches

amethyst: diminishes headaches and dissipates tension

ametrine: treats headaches, tension, and afflictions caused by stress

crystal: diminishes headaches caused by stress

dioptase: relieves pain and nausea from chronic headaches

magnesite: relieves headaches

dark blue sapphire: contributes to the relief of headaches

star sapphire: relieves pain from headaches

serpentine: diminishes headaches

sugilite: alleviates acute pain caused by headaches

Heart

alexandrite: protects against heart problems, contributes to harmonious blood circulation and healthy flow to the brain

green aventurine: soothes, protects, and treats the heart

bloodstone (heliotrope): anchors the energy of the heart

pink chalcedony: strengthens the heart and the immune system

dioptase: prevents coronary and heart disorders, supports one during heart troubles

garnet: purifies, strengthens, and reinforces the blood and heart

pink halite: connects energies of the solar plexus to those of the heart

kunzite: alleviates heart tensions and ailments

rose quartz: reinforces the heart

rhodochrosite: possesses an affinity with the heart chakra

rhodonite: activates the heart chakra and releases blockages

sapphire: supports the circulatory system, the blood, and the vagus nerve

sodalite: encourages the heart to release fears, guilt, and control mechanisms that prevent one from being oneself

Hypertension

apatite: decreases hypertension

hematite: increases the quality of blood and reduces blood pressure

kyanite: decreases blood pressure

lapis lazuli: treats hypertension

malachite: lowers blood pressure

sardonyx: decreases hypertension

sodalite: lowers blood pressure, liberates from mental rigidity, and calms.

Immune System

moss agate: activates the immune system

amethyst: strengthens the immune system

ametrine: reinforces the immune system

andalousite/chiastolite: balances the immune system

aqua aura quartz: reinforces and supports the thymus gland and therefore the immune system

aquamarine: calms excessive reactions of the immune system (such as allergies)

aventurine: stimulates the thymus gland (immune system)

green calcite: reinforces the immune system

blue chalcedony: strengthens the immune system

pink chalcedony: strengthens the heart and immune system

epidote: reinforces the immune system

fluorite: strengthens the immune system

blood jasper (heliotrope), green jasper, yellow jasper: reinforces the immune system

brown jasper: stimulates the immune system

kunzite: stimulates the immune system

lepidolite: strengthens the immune system

malachite: strengthens the immune system

onyx: reinforces the immune system

rhodonite: reinforces the immune system

ruby: strengthens the immune system

sodalite: purifies the lymphatic system and the organs, activating the immune system

tourmaline : stimulates the immune system

zincite: stimulates the immune system

zoisite: strengthens the immune system

Impotence

dark pink beryl (morganite): stimulates sexual energies

carnelian: treats frigidity and impotence

hessonite garnet: treats sterility and impotence

rutilated quartz: guards against impotence

Insecurity

apophyllite: helps to overcome worries and insecurities

smithsonite: calms while penetrating to the heart of patterns related to insecurity

Insomnia

amethyst: relieves insomnia and encourages a restful sleep, decreases nightmares

charoite: relieves insomnia, conferring a deep sleep; brings peaceful sleep to children

chrysoprase: grants a peaceful sleep

coral: relieves insomnia

herkimer diamond: relieves insomnia caused by stress

howlite: acts against insomnia caused by an agitated mind

rose quartz: relieves insomnia

topaz: acts against exhaustion and insomnia

Kidneys

amber: is beneficial for disorders of the kidneys

azurite: supports the kidneys

bloodstone (heliotrope): purifies the kidneys

calcite: supports the kidneys, pancreas, and the spleen

orange calcite: eliminates mucus from the organism and purifies the kidneys

chrysocolla: detoxifies and reinforces the operation of the liver, the kidneys, and intestines

diamond: prevents formation of kidney stones

hematite: supports the role of the kidneys as a blood purifier

jade: eliminates toxins, supports the kidneys

jade-jadeite: regularizes the operation of the kidneys and urinary system

magnetite jade: benefits the kidneys and bladder

nephrite jade: benefits the kidneys (supports the elimination of kidney stones)

brown jasper: purifies the kidneys

lepidolite: strengthens the kidneys

fire opal: contributes to the good performance of the kidneys and adrenal glands

prehnite: treats ailments of the kidneys and urinary incontinence

rose quartz: benefits the kidneys and adrenal glands

rhodochrosite: purifies the circulatory system and kidneys

serpentine: reinforces the kidneys and bladder

sunstone: purifies the kidneys, bladder, and intestines

blue topaz: stimulates renal function

blue tourmaline (indicolite): activates the kidneys and bladder

yellow tourmaline: treats the kidneys

wulfenite: activates renal function and the pancreas

Liver

Botswana agate: stimulates the liver

amazonite: regularizes disorders of the metabolism (liver)

amber: treats skin problems caused by the malfunction of the liver, bile, and metabolism

yellow apatite: treats the liver

azurite: activates and detoxifies the liver

beryl: benefits the liver

bloodstone (heliotrope): detoxifies the liver

carnelian: supports the liver

cat's eye (cymophane): regulates and protects the liver

dendritic chalcedony: detoxifies the liver

charoite: supports the liver and eases damage caused by hepatitis due to excessive alcohol consumption

chrysocolla: detoxifies and reinforces the functioning of the liver

chrysoprase: stimulates the liver

danburite: eases problems of the liver and gallbladder

dioptase: activates the regeneration of the liver

emerald: purifies the liver

epidote: encourages the proper functioning of the liver

yellow fluorite: benefits the liver

almandine, andradite, and uvarovite garnets: benefits the liver and pancreas

Iolite: contributes to the regeneration of the liver

lepidolite: strengthens the liver

malachite: invigorates the liver and purifies toxins

peridot: stimulates the liver and the production of bile

petrified wood: purifies and balances the liver

pietersite: harmonizes the digestive functions, particularly those of the liver

topaz: revitalizes the liver

yellow tourmaline: supports the liver

zircon: stimulates the liver

Lymphatic System

Botswana agate: useful for the assimilation of oxygen, the circulatory system, and the skin

bloodstone (heliotrope): activates the circulation of the lymph and metabolic processes

blue chalcedony: ensures good circulation of the organic fluids (lymph, blood, etc.)

pink chalcedony: activates the circulation of lymph

lazurite: purifies the blood

rose quartz: eliminates impurities from bodily fluids

ruby: detoxifies the blood and the lymph

sodalite: purifies the lymphatic system

sugilite (pale shade): purifies the lymph and blood

Mental Exhaustion

chrysoprase: fights mental exhaustion

fluorite: fights mental exhaustion (a stone for students)

tiger iron: regenerates from mental or emotional exhaustion

Mental Stress

blue lace agate: calms the mind, inviting peace and tranquility

ametrine: releases stress and tension in the head, allowing for better concentration and improved meditation

aquamarine: calms the mind

bloodstone (heliotrope): calms the mind, dissipates confusion, and facilitates decision making

obsidian: eliminates mental stress and tension

sapphire: calms the mind and dissolves intrusive thoughts

blue selenite: allows one to ignore mental chattering during meditation

blue tourmaline (indicolite): calms mental agitation and incessant thoughts

Migraine

aventurine: produces an anti-inflammatory effect, reduces the pain of migraines, and soothes the eyes

clear calcite: eases the tension that causes migraines

dioptase: relieves migraines

hawk eye: soothes migraines

iolite: relieves migraines

jet: soothes migraines

lapis lazuli: alleviates migraines

magnesite: alleviates migraines

rhodochrosite: relieves migraines

blue topaz: eases occipital pains, tightness of the jaw, and migraines

Nervous System

Botswana agate: stimulates the nervous system

amazonite: stimulates the nervous system

amber: regenerates the nervous system

aventurine: benefits the nervous system

pink beryl (morganite): benefits the nervous system

calcite: benefits the nervous system

cat's eye (cymophane): benefits the central nervous system

chrysocolla: helps to maintain proper functioning of the nervous system

epidote: benefits the nervous system

fluorite: supports the activity of the nervous system, in particular that of the brain

jade: balances the nervous system

sapphire: treats disorders of the nervous system

selenite: benefits the entire nervous system

green tourmaline: reinforces the nervous system, bringing greater strength in times of stress and fatigue

Rheumatism

andalusite-chiastolite: treats rheumatism and gout

azurite: relieves symptoms of chronic rheumatism

carnelian: relieves lumbar pains, rheumatism, arthritis, and neuralgia

chalchopyrite: soothes symptoms of rheumatism

copper: relieves symptoms of rheumatism and other ailments related to the joints

emerald: relieves symptoms of rheumatism

garnet: soothes symptoms of rheumatism and arthritis

jet: decreases inflammation, relieves symptoms of arthritis and rheumatism

malachite: contains a high amount of copper, which eases symptoms of rheumatism

turquoise: neutralizes hyperacidity and treats rheumatism.

Sciatic Nerve

red calcite: relieves lower back pain; treats the sciatic nerve, the hips, legs, and knees

copper: decreases inflammation and pain

lepidolite: relieves neuralgia and pain in the sciatic nerve and joints

magnetite: decreases inflammation

Sexuality

fire agate: stimulates vitality on all levels, including sexual

orange calcite: treats overall problems of the reproductive system, stimulates the libido

carnelian: stimulates sexuality and creativity

dendritic chalcedony: decreases inflammation of the female sex organs

coral (orange): increases the libido, particularly for men garnet: balances sexual desires

hessonite garnet: balances overactive sexual desire

pyrope garnet: revitalizes the sex organs

rhodolite garnet: encourages a healthy sexuality

red garnet: increases the libido

spessartite garnet: to be used in moderation, treats sexual imbalances, blockages, and repressions; neutralizes guilt due to conservative conditioning and negative experiences

hawk eye: alleviates an overly active libido

malachite: known as the midwife stone, facilitates childbirth, vibrates with the female sex organs and treats any sexual discomfort

fire opal: stimulates the libido and encourages spontaneous pleasure

pietersite: balances the production of hormones governing the reproductive system

rose quartz: reinforces the sex organs

rhodochrosite: awakens the libido by reinvigorating the sex organs, removes blockages caused by sexual abuse

ruby: increases the libido

sphene (or titanite): a good sexual stimulant for men

sunstone: helps for all disorders of the reproductive organs

zincite: alights the fires of creativity and sexuality, treats infertility

zoisite: encourages fertility and stimulates the sexual energies

Sinusitis

aquamarine: relieves the symptoms of sinusitis

aventurine: benefits the sinuses

charoite: purifies the sinuses

chrysocolla: reduces inflammation of the sinuses, amygdala, larynx, and lungs

emerald: treats the sinuses and lungs

fluorite: treats the symptoms of sinusitis and influenza

iolite: supports the sinuses and respiratory system

phenacite: relieves congested sinuses

clear blue sapphire: relieves congested sinuses

blue tourmaline (indicolite): treats the symptoms of sinusitis

Sterility (see also Sexuality)

carnelian: acts against sterility and impotence during physico-energetic blockages of the reproductive organs

chrysoprase: treats sterility caused by infection

hessonite garnet: helps to treat sterility and impotence

Steroids

tiger iron: secretes natural steroids

Stress

apophyllite: decreases stress

aqua aura quartz: eliminates aggressiveness and frailty due to stress

aquamarine: diffuses a calming energy that alleviates stress

aragonite: useful in periods of stress

aventurine: calms emotional stress and treats insomnia

beryl: encourages constructive stress management

golden beryl: relieves emotional nervousness eases anxiety during stressful circumstances and an overload of work

calcite: calms fears and reduces stress

blue calcite: reduces stress, anxiety, and negativity

green calcite: reduces stress and calms heart palpitations

cat's eye (cymophane): alleviates stress

celestite: contributes to maintaining a harmonious atmosphere in times of stress

blue chalcedony: eliminates stress, an ideal stone for students

dendritic chalcedony: invites calm and poise in moments of stress or when facing confrontation with others

charoite: alleviates stress and worry

chrysocolla: eases digestive problems due to the stress (such as ulcers)

dioptase: fights addictions and stress

epidote: supports regeneration following disease or burnout

fluorite: decreases stress

hematite: helps to reduce stress

jasper: gives support during times of stress

kyanite: reduces stress

lapis lazuli: reduces stress

lepidolite: reduces stress

rainbow obsidian: alleviates stress

white opal: alleviates worry and chronic stress

peridot: alleviates stress

rhodochrosite: reduces stress and treats stress-related ailments such as gastric ulcers

serpentine: calms the nervous system

sunstone: dissipates stress, anxiety, and fear

blue tiger eye: reduces stress

black tourmaline: supports one during times of stress

green tourmaline: alleviates stress

Tendinitis

azurite: relieves tendinitis and alleviates muscle and bone pain

Tennis Elbow

magnetite: decreases joint pains, neuralgia of the arm, and symptoms of tennis elbow

Throat

blue lace agate: known as a powerful healer of the throat

amber: is beneficial for ailments of the throat

blue apatite: purifies and activates the throat chakra

aqua aura quartz: stimulates the throat chakra

aquamarine: stimulates, activates, and purifies the throat chakra; treats sore throats

aventurine: benefits the throat

azurite: eases problems of the throat

beryl: treats infections of the throat, especially when taken in the form of an elixir

blue calcite: relieves inflammation of the throat

blue chalcedony: activates the throat chakra and treats disorders of the throat

chrysocolla: fights infections, in particular of the throat and amygdala; treats inflammation of the sinuses, amygdala, larynx, and lungs

blue fluorite: balances the throat chakra

melanite garnet: dissolves blockages of the throat

pyrope garnet: alleviates sore throats

blue halite: relieves blockages of the throat

hawk eye: activates the throat chakra

kyanite: strengthens the throat chakra

larimar: alleviates sore throats

rhodonite: alleviates streptococcal infections of the throat

sodalite: reinforces treatments of the throat, vocal cords, the larynx, and during times of persistent hoarseness

sunstone: soothes chronically sore throats

tiger eye: treats throat problems

blue topaz: eases problems related to the throat

blue tourmaline (indicolite): eases disorders of the throat

turquoise: purifies the throat chakra and soothes sore throats

wulfenite: treats chronically sore throats

Thymus

amazonite: harmonizes the thymus

aqua aura quartz: reinforces and supports the thymus gland and therefore the immune system.

aventurine: benefits the thymus

green calcite: stimulates the thymus gland

chrysoprase: reinforces the thymus

citrine: activates the thymus

diamond: reinforces the thymus thereby strengthening the immune system

dioptase: activates the thymus

peridot: improves the functioning of the thymus

prehnite: alleviates ailments of the thymus gland

Thyroid

amazonite: supports the thyroid and the parathyroid glands

amber: balances the thyroid

aquamarine: harmonizes the thyroid gland

azurite: benefits the thyroid

blue calcite: relieves inflammation of the thyroid

chrysocolla: regulates the thyroid

epidote: supports the thyroid gland

hawk eye: benefits the thyroid

kyanite: supports the thyroid and the parathyroid glands

lapis lazuli: activates the thyroid

malachite: balances the thyroid gland

rhodochrosite: balances the thyroid

rutile: balances the thyroid

RESOURCES

ENGLISH

Melody. *Love is in the Earth.* Wheat Ridge, CO: Earth-Love Publishing House, 1995.

Raphaell, Katrina. *Crystal Healing.* Vol 2. Santa Fe, NM: Aurora Press, 1987.

FRENCH

Basevi, Tabish. *Cristallothérapie.* Paris: Éditions de Vecchi, 2003.

Coquet, Michel. *Les pierres précieuses (dans la science des sept rayons).*

Da Ros, Serge, *Les énergies bénéfiques des pierres & cristaux.* Paris: Éditions Trajectoire, 2002.

Gienger, Michael. *Manuel de lithothérapie, ou l'art de se soigner avec les pierres.* Paris: Éditions Véga, 2005.

Hall, Judy. *La Bible des Cristaux.* Paris: Guy Trédaniel Éditeur, 2004.

Paulin, Jean-Yves. *La Mystique des Pierres.* Lyon, France: Éditions du Cosmogone, 2002.

Seno, Jean-Jacques. *Manuel de lithothérapie.* Puiseaux, France: Pardès, 2003.

Tetteroo, Tosca. *Pierres et Cristaux.* Montpellier, France Éditions Gange, 1995.

Personal Notes

ABOUT THE AUTHORS

Collaborating in this present work are the members of The Group of 5. This name, The Group of 5, evokes the five-branch star symbolizing the perfect person, drawn by Leonardo da Vinci, a visionary of his time. It also refers to therapists affiliated with the Medicine Buddha Mandala Institute of Applied Alternative Therapies. We are united within this star and form a working unity in service to all.

Listed below are the names of those who have collaborated on the present volume: Klaire D. Roy, Lisa Corbeil, Richard Frappier, André Lavoie, Gisèle Lavoie, Kristiane Roy, Jacqueline Sylvain, and Marcel Tardif.

CRYSTALS AND STONES

Publications by Paume de Saint-Germain Publishing

The Lion's Roar: The Master from Montreal, Klaire D. Roy, 2008.

New Tantrism, Klaire D. Roy, 2008.

Tantric Training in the Age of Ray 7, Klaire D. Roy, 2008.

New Tantrism: Introductory Themes, Klaire D. Roy, 2007.

Conclave of the Cryptic 7, Volume I, Klaire D. Roy, 2007.

The Spiritual Science of Essential Yoga: Techniques of Meditation, Mantrams, and Invocations, Volume I, Sri Adi Dadi, compiled by Martine G. Fortier, 2004.

Publications by North Atlantic Books

The Book of Stones: Who They Are and What They Teach, Robert Simmons and Naisha Ahsian

Stones of the New Consciousness: Healing, Awakening and Co-creating with Crystals, Minerals and Gems, Robert Simmons

The Mysterious Story of X7: Exploring the Spiritual Nature of Matter, Anonymous, Robert Sardello, Sir George Trevelyan, and Anne K. Edwards

Steps on the Stone Path: Working with Crystals and Minerals as a Spiritual Practice, Robert Sardello